WHAT A YEAR IT WAS!

1968

A walk back in time...

4/5/2008

To Creech Hanes

From Elizabeth

Media

Dedicated to America's Vietnam-era veterans,
with gratitude for their sacrifices.

Publishers • Lawrence Siegel & Art Worthington
Designers • Peter Hess & Liz Howard
Writing & Research • Peter Hess & Debbie Sedley
Facilitator • Pamela Thomas
Series originated by Beverly Cohn

www.FLICKBACK.com
(800) 541-3533

Contents

Arts & Entertainment

Peter O'Toole and **Katharine Hepburn** pair for the Plantagenet drama, *The Lion in Winter.* He is philandering King Henry II, consumed with establishing his succession amid familial intrigue. She plays his embittered wife, Eleanor of Aquitaine, recently released from prison. Their performances gain Academy Award nominations for both. Hepburn will win her record-breaking third Best Actress Oscar®; Peter O'Toole does not win, but will eventually earn the distinction of being the most-nominated actor (8) to never capture the coveted statue.

Movies

The COUNTER CULTURE Goes MAINSTREAM

Big studios and independents alike rush to catch a piece of the sex, drugs and rock 'n roll action ignited by 1967's "Summer of Love." The documentary ***Monterey Pop*** vividly captures headline performers in their glory at the granddaddy of all rock festivals—the one that started it all.

French New Wave auteur **Jean-Luc Godard** weighs in with ***Sympathy for the Devil***, which incorporates a **Rolling Stones** recording session among a confusing chain of events. Stones front man **Mick Jagger** figures again as a reclusive rock star in director **Nicolas Roeg**'s decadent ***Performance***. **The Beatles**, or at least their animated representatives, fight off Blue Meanies in ***Yellow Submarine***'s psychedelic cartoon Pepperland. Underground comic characters spring to life in ***Barbarella*** — in which **Jane Fonda** creates a sensation with a sexy space striptease — and Italy's ***Danger: Diabolik***.

In a twist, ***Head***, the feature film debut of the fluffy TV pop group **The Monkees**, actually earns the quartet some belated critical plaudits.

Lower-profile entries in the counterculture derby include ***Wild in the Streets***, ***You Are What You Eat***, ***Alice in Acidland*** and ***Psych-Out*** ("come where the pleasure lovers are").

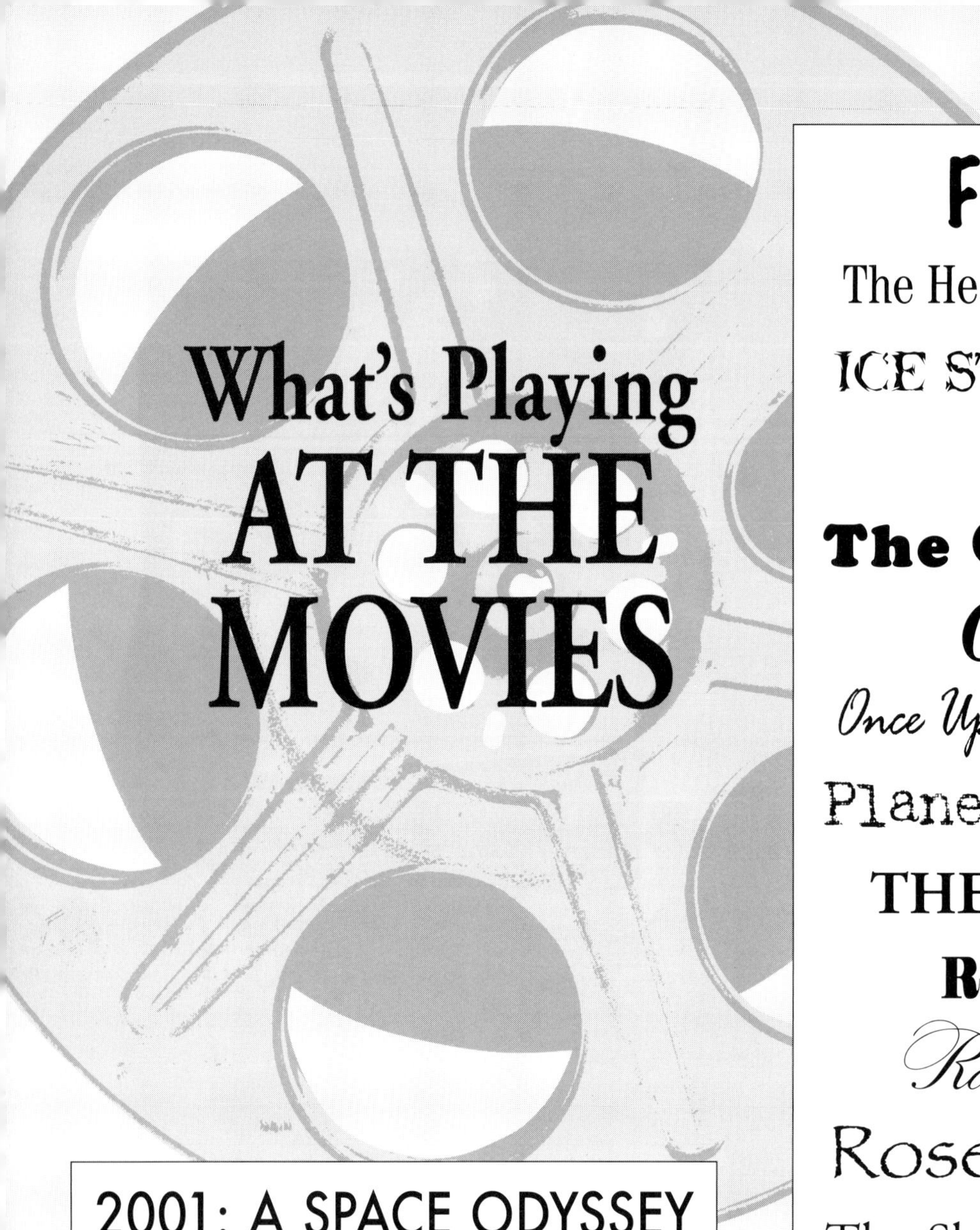

What's Playing AT THE MOVIES

Funny Girl
The Heart Is a Lonely Hunter
ICE STATION ZEBRA
Isadora
The Odd Couple
OLIVER!
Once Upon a Time in the West
Planet of the Apes
THE PRODUCERS
Rachel, Rachel
Romeo and Juliet
Rosemary's Baby
The Shoes of the Fisherman
Star!
STAY AWAY, JOE
The Subject Was Roses
THE THOMAS CROWN AFFAIR
War and Peace
WHERE EAGLES DARE
YOURS, MINE AND OURS

2001: A SPACE ODYSSEY
Bandolero!
BULLITT
CHARLY
CHITTY CHITTY BANG BANG
The Detective
THE DEVIL'S BRIGADE
FACES
Finian's Rainbow

The WILLIAM WYLER-RAY STARK Production
FUNNY GIRL
People who see Funny Girl again are the luckiest people in the world!

MGM PRESENTS A STANLEY KUBRICK PRODUCTION
2001: a space odyssey
STARRING
KEIR DULLEA · GARY LOCKWOOD
SCREENPLAY BY
STANLEY KUBRICK AND ARTHUR C. CLARKE
PRODUCED AND DIRECTED BY
STANLEY KUBRICK
SUPERPANAVISION® AND METROCOLOR
MGM

Mia Farrow
In a William Castle Production
Rosemary's Baby

AN UNUSUAL AND IMPORTANT MOTION PICTURE FROM THE PEN OF PIERRE BOULLE, AUTHOR OF "THE BRIDGE ON THE RIVER KWAI"
20th CENTURY-FOX PRESENTS
CHARLTON HESTON
in
AN ARTHUR P. JACOBS PRODUCTION
PLANET OF THE APES

The word 'cop' isn't written all over him-someth
STEVE McQUEEN AS 'BULLITT'
A SOLAR PRODUCTION
Not many freaky cops like BULLITT around. You look at the Italian shoes and the turtleneck and you have to wonder. You listen to the official beefs about "personal misconduct," "disruptive influence," you figure he's got to be up for trade.
But when some rare Chicago blood starts spilling in San Fransisco, they give BULLITT the mop. They weren't exactly doing him a favor. But they've done a great big one for you.
ROBERT VAUGHN
JAQUELINE BISSET · DON GORDON · ROBERT DUVALL · SIMON OAKLAND · NORMAN FELL

PARAMOUNT PICTURES presents
Jack Lemmon and Walter Matthau are The Odd Couple
...say no more.

The Academy Awards

Oscars® Presented in 1968

Rod Steiger

BEST PICTURE
IN THE HEAT OF THE NIGHT

BEST ACTOR
ROD STEIGER,
In the Heat of the Night

BEST ACTRESS
KATHARINE HEPBURN,
Guess Who's Coming to Dinner

BEST DIRECTOR
MIKE NICHOLS,
The Graduate

BEST SUPPORTING ACTOR
GEORGE KENNEDY, *Cool Hand Luke*

BEST SUPPORTING ACTRESS
ESTELLE PARSONS, *Bonnie and Clyde*

BEST SONG
"TALK TO THE ANIMALS," *Doctor Dolittle*

1968 Favorites (Oscars® Presented in 1969)

Barbra Streisand

BEST PICTURE
OLIVER!

BEST ACTOR
CLIFF ROBERTSON, *Charly*

BEST ACTRESS (TIE)
KATHARINE HEPBURN,
The Lion in Winter
BARBRA STREISAND, *Funny Girl*

BEST DIRECTOR
CAROL REED, *Oliver!*

BEST SUPPORTING ACTOR
JACK ALBERTSON, *The Subject Was Roses*

BEST SUPPORTING ACTRESS
RUTH GORDON, *Rosemary's Baby*

BEST SONG
"THE WINDMILLS OF YOUR MIND,"
The Thomas Crown Affair

The 40th annual Academy Awards ceremony, hosted by **Bob Hope** at the Santa Monica Civic Auditorium on April 10, 1968, is postponed from Monday the 8th due to the assassination of Dr. Martin Luther King, Jr.

Bob Hope circa 1960

Director **Alfred Hitchcock** receives the Academy's special Irving G. Thalberg Memorial Award.

Alfred Hitchcock

In 1969, the 41st Academy Awards ceremonies would move to the brand new Dorothy Chandler Pavilion of the Music Center of Los Angeles County, and be the first to be telecast to 37 nations worldwide.

NEW STARS of '68

Timothy **Dalton**
Faye **Dunaway**
Anthony **Hopkins**
Vanessa **Redgrave**
Cliff **Robertson**

Anthony Hopkins

Faye Dunaway

TOP GROSSING FILMS North America

1. *The Graduate*
2. *Guess Who's Coming to Dinner*
3. *Bonnie and Clyde*
4. *Valley of the Dolls*
5. *The Odd Couple*
6. *Planet of the Apes*
7. *Rosemary's Baby*
8. *The Jungle Book*
9. *Yours, Mine and Ours*

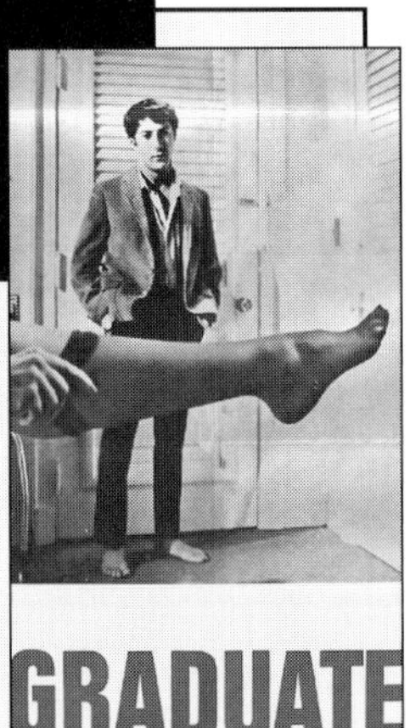

GOLDEN GLOBE AWARDS

Presented in 1969

BEST PICTURE (Drama)
The Lion in Winter

BEST PICTURE (Musical or Comedy)
Oliver!

ACTOR in a Leading Role (Drama)
Peter O'Toole
The Lion in Winter

ACTOR in a Leading Role (Musical or Comedy)
Ron Moody
Oliver!

ACTRESS in a Leading Role (Drama)
Joanne Woodward
Rachel, Rachel

ACTRESS in a Leading Role (Musical or Comedy)
Barbra Streisand
Funny Girl

SUPPORTING ACTOR
Daniel Massey
Star!

SUPPORTING ACTRESS
Ruth Gordon
Rosemary's Baby

DIRECTOR
Paul Newman
Rachel, Rachel

Short Takes

Steve McQueen reigns as one of Hollywood's most bankable stars, and he enjoys another big year with two hit films.

Steve McQueen

The gritty cop drama ***Bullitt*** has McQueen in hot pursuit of a mob boss responsible for the murder of a protected witness. The ensuing car chase through the streets of San Francisco casts the mold for high-speed action sequences for years to come. Two modified Mustangs and two Dodge Chargers are used for the scenes, with only a single Mustang surviving the punishing shoot. The 10-minute sequence takes three weeks to film, with speeds approaching 110 mph. The movie is also notable as the first mainstream Hollywood production to include the expletive "Bullshit!"

The Thomas Crown Affair centers on a bank heist and the romantic entanglement between the suspect (McQueen) and an insurance investigator (**Faye Dunaway**). **Sean Connery** and **Eva Marie Saint** are the initial choices for the respective roles. Connery rejects the part, a decision he later regrets, and *The Thomas Crown Affair* comes to be Steve McQueen's favorite work. The film is also justly famous for French composer **Michel Legrand**'s lush musical score.

Oliver!'s *Jack Wild, Ron Moody, Mark Lester*

Oliver!, one of the year's biggest hits, is a musical adaptation of the **Charles Dickens** classic novel *Oliver Twist.* Pre-production rumors have **Richard Burton** and **Elizabeth Taylor** participating, as well as **Laurence Harvey** and **Peter Sellers**. None do, and the story films with its original stage cast—including **Ron Moody** and **Jack Wild**—largely intact. The huge production covers six London sound stages and an entire studio backlot, and goes on to nab five Academy Awards.

Omar Sharif

Another musical, ***Funny Girl***, features **Barbra Streisand** reprising her Broadway role as entertainer **Fanny Brice**, with **Omar Sharif** as the male lead. **Shirley MacLaine** is the studio's first choice for the Brice part, but producer **Ray Stark** insists on Streisand, and Streisand herself later nixes **Frank Sinatra** in favor of Sharif. Neither a turbulent set nor changing directors keep *Funny Girl* from scoring multiple awards, including an Oscar® for Streisand.

Memorable Lines

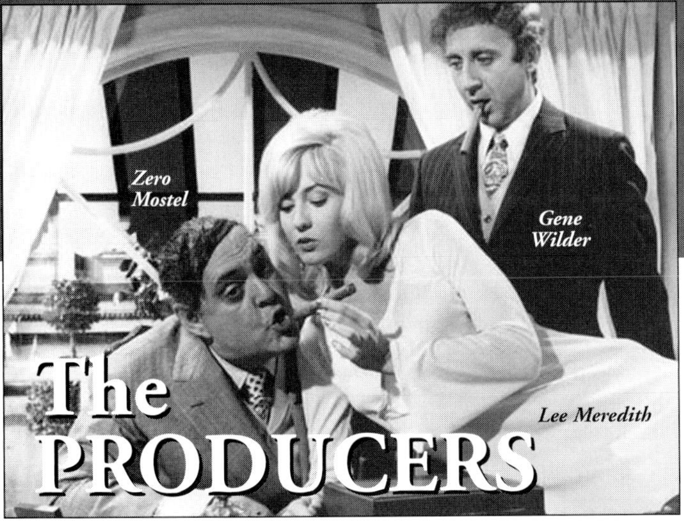

Max Bialystock: *Shut up, I'm having a rhetorical conversation.*

Max Bialystock: *That's exactly why we want to produce this play. To show the world the true Hitler, the Hitler you loved, the Hitler you knew, the Hitler with a song in his heart.*

Max Bialystock: *How could this happen? I was so careful. I picked the wrong play, the wrong director, the wrong cast. Where did I go right?*

The Odd Couple

Oscar Madison: *I can't take it anymore, Felix, I'm cracking up. Everything you do irritates me. And when you're not here, the things I know you're gonna do when you come in irritate me. You leave me little notes on my pillow. Told you 158 times I can't stand little notes on my pillow. "We're all out of cornflakes. F.U." Took me three hours to figure out F.U. was Felix Ungar!*

Felix Ungar: *In other words, you're throwing me out.*
Oscar Madison: *Not in other words. Those are the perfect ones!*

Richard Forst: *What do you want to drink?*
Maria Forst: *Well, whatever it is, I want it on the rocks, straight and dirty, because I feel very, very bitchy tonight.*
Richard Forst: *Well, I feel very, very bitchy too. That makes two of us.*

Maria Forst: *There's a Bergman film in the neighborhood.*
Richard Forst: *I don't feel like getting depressed tonight.*

Charly Gordon: *My name is Charly Gordon and I live in a room, and I got no sister and no dog, and I am stupid!*

Charly Gordon: *I was wondering why the people who would never dream of laughing at a blind or a crippled man would laugh at a moron?*

HORROR *and* SCI-FI

An underwhelming number of science fiction and horror entries are released in the year, but some that see the light of day create a significant impact. Gothic shocker ***Rosemary's Baby***, with its excellent production values and top-notch performances by **Mia Farrow** as a horrified expectant mother and **John Cassavettes** as her beleaguered husband, raises the bar for all future spawn-of-the-devil entries.

Stanley Kubrick's mystical and elegiac ***2001: A Space Odyssey*** transcends the sci-fi genre to pose timeless questions about who we are, whence we came, and what awaits us. Anyone who has seen the chilling sequences featuring the disembodied voice of HAL-9000, the onboard computer that attempts to wrest control of a spacecraft from its crew, has had the seeds of doubt permanently planted in their mind regarding the future of man's relationship to machines.

In ***Planet of the Apes***, a glistening **Charlton Heston** learns the hard way that, in some places, *Homo sapiens* is not top dog. It's a movie with much to answer for, since it spawns a cottage industry of sequels and merchandise, with the franchise claiming many adherents still.

George Romero's low-budget ***Night of the Living Dead*** reigns supreme as the king of all zombie flicks. Its undead inhabitants lumbering in stark black and white make such an impression that the film comes to reside in the National Film Registry of the Library of Congress.

Not to be confused with Romero's minor masterpiece is ***Astro Zombies***, most likely to be encountered at a drive-in near you. A leering **Vincent Price** is the Witchfinder General (its original British title) in American International's ***The Conqueror Worm***. And those loud Japanese reptiles—Godzilla, Rodan, et al—are at it again, this time staging a summit in ***Destroy All Monsters***.

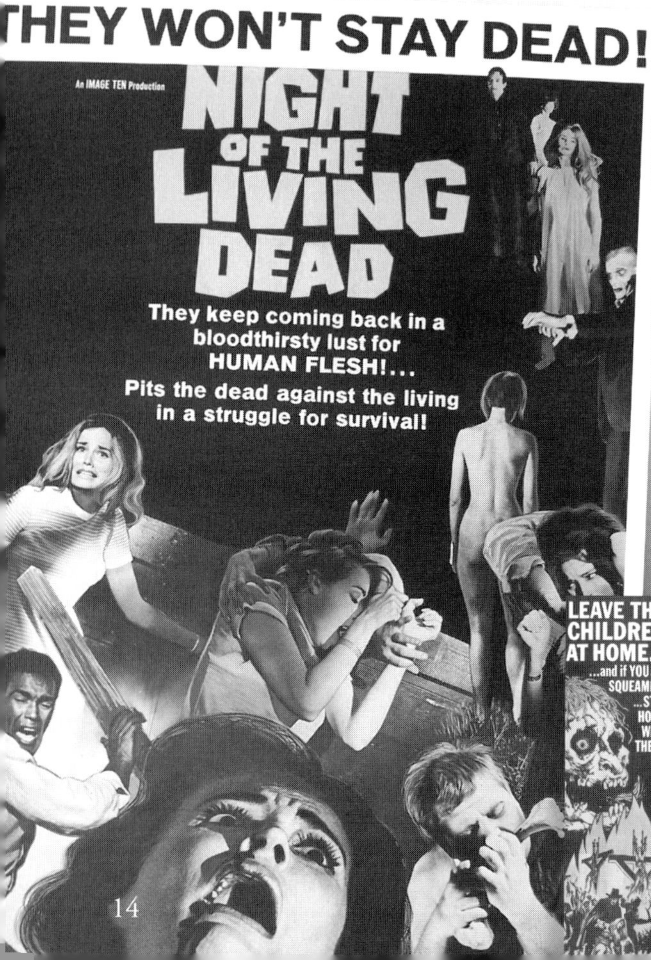

BORN IN 1968 ★

DANIEL CRAIG ★ BRENDAN FRASER ★ ANTHONY MICHAEL HALL ★ LUCY LIU ★ MOLLY RINGWALD ★ GUY RITCHIE ★ JOHN SINGLETON ★ NAOMI WATTS

Lucy Liu

John Singleton

Hollywood Bids a Fond Farewell

KAY FRANCIS - Film actress notable for her performances in *The Cocoanuts* and *Trouble in Paradise.*

RAMON NOVARRO (69) - Dashing silent screen actor who achieved the height of his popularity in *Ben-Hur.*

Ramon Novarro

1968 ADVERTISEMENT

FIRST...BY WESTINGHOUSE
INSTANT-ON® TV

COMPARE...YOU'LL BUY WESTINGHOUSE!

First by Westinghouse, instant sound and picture... no waiting for sound or picture to warm-up. Gives added component life and reliability to Westinghouse television.

Once again Westinghouse engineering and constant leadership give you the fine quality and performance you expect from the leader.

You can be sure if it's Westinghouse

Television

Vaudeville collides with flower power and the result is *Laugh-In*, which weekly surrounds hosts **Dan Rowan** and **Dick Martin** with a large ensemble spouting rapid-fire political and sexual gags interspersed with gyrating bikini dances on graffiti-inspired sets. Irreverent skits feature an array of revolving characters including a Nazi named Wolfgang, a priest, and a prude on a park bench. Many of the show's nonsensical quips—"You bet your sweet bippy"; "Look that up in your Funk and Wagnall's"— attain water-cooler currency. A galaxy of guest stars join in the hilarity and *Laugh-In* launches a number of its regulars into show-biz orbit, including **Lily Tomlin** and **Goldie Hawn**.

Clockwise from top left, cast members Jo Anne Worley, Artie Johnson, Lily Tomlin, Henry Gibson, Dick Martin, Dan Rowan, Goldie Hawn, and Judy Carne.

QUIETLY SHAKING THINGS UP

Diahann Carroll stars in *Julia*, the first weekly sitcom to depict an African American woman in a non-stereotypical leading role. Though Carroll's Julia Baker, a widowed nurse, promotes a positive image of an attractive, hardworking mother struggling to raise a son in a middle-class environment, the show is criticized by some segments of the African American community for not being "black enough" and for presenting an inaccurate picture of black reality in America. Carroll's work in *Julia* earns her a Best Female TV Star Golden Globe award.

NEW on TV

Here Come the Brides

Frontier lumberjacks Bobby Sherman, Robert Brown, David Soul

The Mod Squad

Clarence Williams III (top), Michael Cole and Peggy Lipton star as undercover cops.

Hawaii Five-0

Jack Lord is island cop Steve McGarrett. "Book 'em, Danno!"

Here's Lucy

Sitcom queen Lucille Ball returns as a single mom.

The Doris Day Show

The versatile star comes to TV as a widowed career mom living on a suburban ranch.

Mayberry R.F.D.

The Andy Griffith Show *sans Andy. Ken Berry (center top) heads the cast.*

PRIMETIME LINEUP

		7:00	7:30	8:00	8:30	9:00	9:30	10:00	10:30
SATURDAY	ABC	Local	The Dating Game	The Newlywed Game	Lawrence Welk Show		The Hollywood Palace		Local
	CBS	Local	Jackie Gleason Show		My Three Sons	Hogan's Heroes	Petticoat Junction	Mannix	
	NBC	Local	Adam-12	Get Smart	The Ghost and Mrs. Muir	Saturday Night at the Movies			
SUNDAY	ABC	Land of the Giants		The FBI		The ABC Sunday Night Movie			
	CBS	Local	Gentle Ben	Ed Sullivan Show		Smothers Brothers Comedy Hour		Mission: Impossible	
	NBC	Local	Walt Disney's Wonderful World of Color		Mothers-in-Law	Bonanza		Beautiful Phyllis Diller Show	
MONDAY	ABC	Local	The Avengers		Peyton Place	The Outcasts		The Big Valley	
	CBS	Local	Gunsmoke		Here's Lucy	Mayberry RFD	Family Affair	Carol Burnett Show	
	NBC	Local	I Dream of Jeannie	Rowan and Martin's Laugh-In		NBC Monday Night at the Movies			
TUESDAY	ABC	Local	The Mod Squad		It Takes a Thief		N.Y.P.D.	That's Life	
	CBS	Local	Lancer		Red Skelton Hour		Doris Day Show	CBS News Hour alt. w/ 60 Minutes	
	NBC	Local	Jerry Lewis Show		Julia	NBC Tuesday Night at the Movies			
WEDNESDAY	ABC	Local	Here Come the Brides		Peyton Place	The ABC Wednesday Night Movie and Specials			
	CBS	Local	Daktari		The Good Guys	The Beverly Hillbillies	Green Acres	Jonathan Winters Show	
	NBC	Local	The Virginian			The Kraft Music Hall		The Outsider	
THURSDAY	ABC	Local	The Ugliest Girl in Town	The Flying Nun	Bewitched	That Girl	Journey to the Unknown		Local
	CBS	Local	Blondie	Hawaii Five-O		The CBS Thursday Night Movies			
	NBC	Local	Daniel Boone		Ironside		Dragnet 1969	Dean Martin Show	
FRIDAY	ABC	Local	Operation: Entertainment		The Felony Squad	Don Rickles Show	The Guns of Will Sonnett	Judd, for the Defense	
	CBS	Local	The Wild, Wild West		Gomer Pyle, USMC	The CBS Friday Night Movies			
	NBC	Local	The High Chaparral		The Name of the Game			Star Trek	

Squeezing The Smothers

At the start of the 1968–69 season, CBS demands that the controversial ***Smothers Brothers Comedy Hour*** shows be finished 10 days early so the censors have time to edit. In the season premiere, CBS cuts a segment of **Harry Belafonte** singing against a backdrop of chaos during the 1968 Democratic National Convention. Censorship battles continue throughout the year, including debate over a **David Steinberg** bit about Moses and the Burning Bush.

Dick and Tom Smothers sandwich guest Inger Stevens.

- **Elvis Presley**'s '68 Comeback Special airs on NBC.
- **The Lennon Sisters** make their final appearance on *The Lawrence Welk Show.*
- **Joan Crawford** makes a guest appearance for five episodes on the soap opera *The Secret Storm,* filling in for her ailing daughter, **Christina**. However, Joan slurs her lines and appears intoxicated during the live broadcast.

The long-running TV news-magazine 60 MINUTES debuts in September, alternating with CBS News specials. MIKE WALLACE and HARRY REASONER host.

Mike Wallace

Race Matters

When British singer **Petula Clark** touches guest star **Harry Belafonte** on the arm during her television special, the show's sponsor raises concerns about the interracial contact. The scene airs intact at Clark's insistence and the show garners good ratings.

Amid widespread black rioting following the assassination of **Martin Luther King, Jr.**, the Boston concert performance of soul singer **James Brown** is televised in the hope that the broadcast will help quell further violence. A number of incidents are apparently forestalled.

Harry Belafonte

The first interracial kiss to air on U.S. television is shared between **William Shatner** and **Nichelle Nichols** during the *Star Trek* episode "Plato's Stepchildren."

James Brown

Shatner and Nichols—Star Trek's Captain Kirk and Uhura.

BORN IN 1968 ★

GILLIAN ANDERSON
GARY COLEMAN
LUCY LAWLESS
WENDI PETERS

Gillian Anderson

Say Goodbye to...

The Andy Griffith Show
Lost in Space
Batman
The Monkees
The Prisoner

Nielsen's Top Twenty

1. Rowan & Martin's Laugh-In
2. Gomer Pyle, U.S.M.C.
3. Bonanza
4. Mayberry R.F.D.
5. Family Affair
6. Gunsmoke
7. Julia
8. The Dean Martin Show
9. Here's Lucy
10. The Beverly Hillbillies
11. Mission: Impossible
12. Bewitched
13. The Red Skelton Hour
14. My Three Sons
15. The Glen Campbell Goodtime Hour
16. Ironside
17. The Virginian
18. The F.B.I.
19. Green Acres
20. Dragnet

Red Skelton

1968 - 1969 EMMY awards

Best Drama Series
NET Playhouse

Best Actor in a Drama Series
Carl Betz
Judd for the Defense

Best Actress in a Drama Series
Barbara Bain
Mission: Impossible

Best Supporting Actor in a Drama Series
Milburn Stone
Gunsmoke

Best Supporting Actress in a Drama Series
Susan St. James
The Name of the Game

Best Comedy Series
Get Smart

Best Actor in a Comedy Series
Don Adams
Get Smart

Best Actress in a Comedy Series
Hope Lange
The Ghost and Mrs. Muir

Fans erupt in angry protest when NBC breaks away from a live pro football game to air a TV movie adaptation of *Heidi*.

Radio

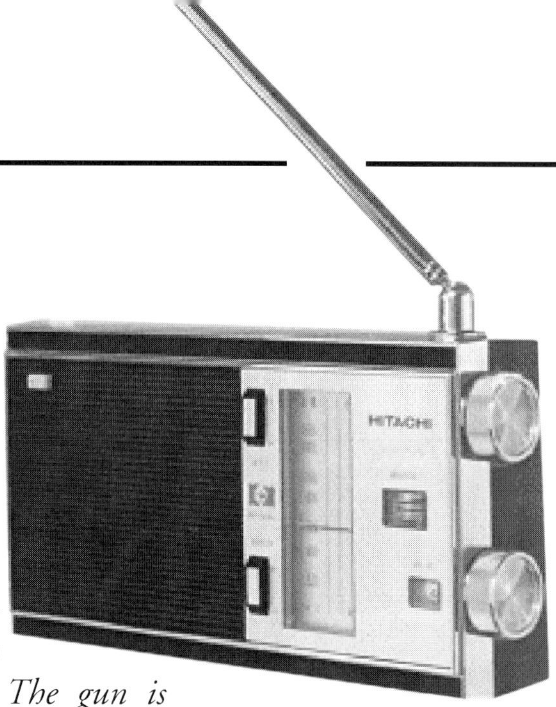

When Senator Robert F. Kennedy is assassinated in June, Andrew West of the Mutual Broadcasting System (MBS) is standing right behind him. His tape, with the famous words, *"He still has the gun! The gun is pointed at me right this moment! Get the gun!"* is broadcast by all three television networks and thousands of radio stations worldwide.

John Charles Daly, well-known as the host of *What's My Line* for 17 years, resigns as head of the U.S. Information Agency's Voice of America after only one year.

Radio Commentator **Westbrook Van Voorhis**, best known as the voice of *The March of Time* from 1931-1953, dies of cancer at the age of 64.

ABC announces that **Don McNeill**'s *Breakfast Club* will end after 35 years.

In a Gallup Poll commissioned by the National Association of Broadcasters, 87% of those polled name news reports as their "primary preference in radio broadcasts," followed by music, sports, current events, personality interviews, and religion.

- The FCC imposes a freeze on applications for AM radio stations.
- In April, the FCC approves the first one million dollar FM sale: WDBN-FM, in Medina, Ohio.
- An attempt to establish Free Radio Andorra fails.

Billboard's TOP 20

1. *Hey Jude* - The Beatles
2. *I Heard It Through The Grapevine* - Marvin Gaye
3. *Love Is Blue* - Paul Mauriat
4. *Honey* - Bobby Goldsboro
5. *People Got To Be Free* - The Rascals
6. *(Sittin' On) The Dock Of the Bay* - Otis Redding
7. *This Guy's In love With You* - Herb Alpert
8. *Mrs. Robinson* - Simon & Garfunkel
9. *Love Child* - Diana Ross & The Supremes
10. *Tighten Up* - Archie Bell & The Drells
11. *Hello, I Love You* - The Doors
12. *Judy In Disguise (With Glasses)* - John Fred & His Playboy Band
13. *Grazing In the Grass* - Hugh Masekela
14. *Harper Valley P.T.A.* - Jeannie C. Riley
15. *Green Tambourine* - The Lemon Pipers
16. *(Theme From) The Valley of The Dolls* - Dionne Warwick
17. *Young Girl* - the Union Gap featuring Gary Puckett
18. *Those Were The Days* - Mary Hopkin
19. *The Horse* - Cliff Nobles & Company
20. *Born To Be Wild* - Steppenwolf

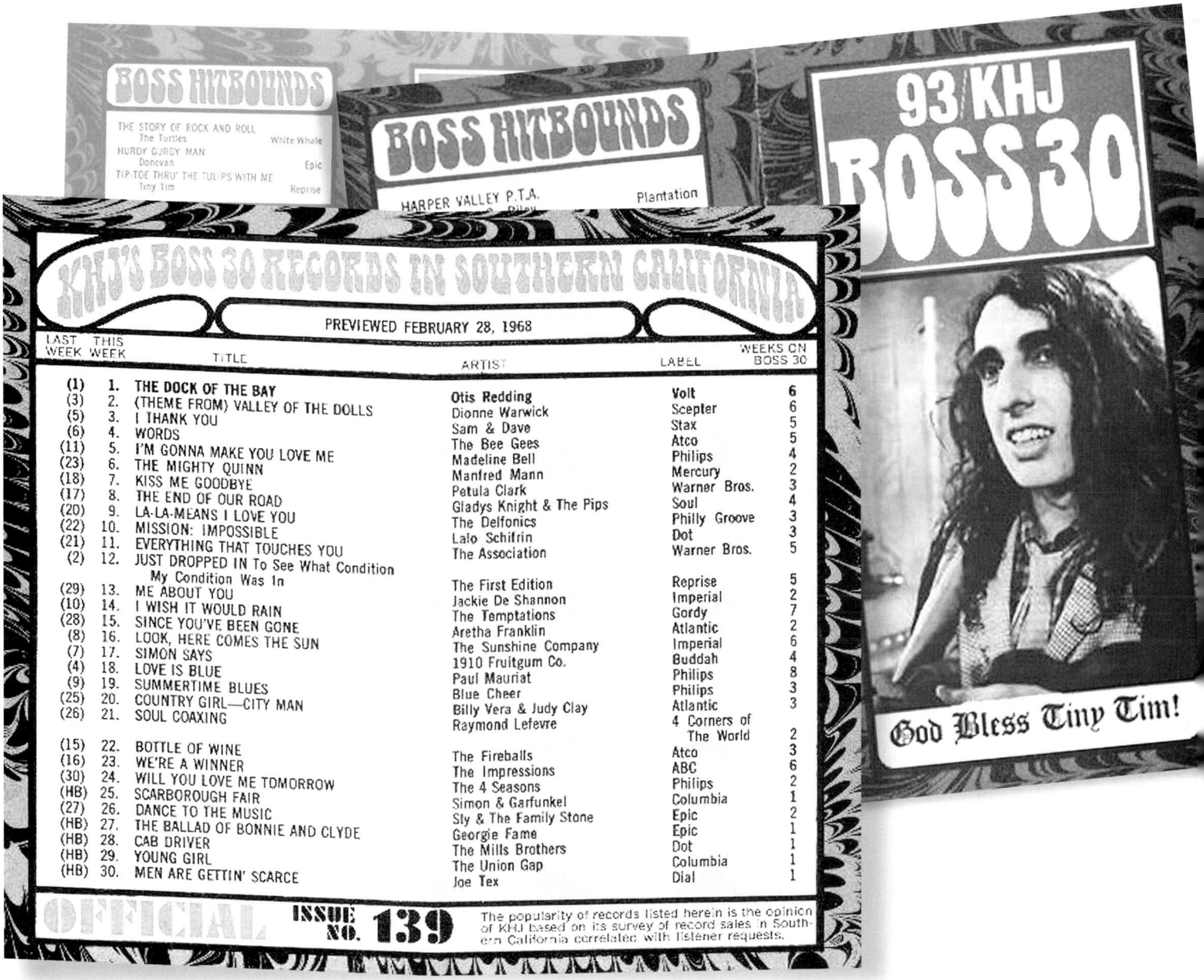

KHJ'S BOSS 30 RECORDS IN SOUTHERN CALIFORNIA

PREVIEWED FEBRUARY 28, 1968

LAST WEEK	THIS WEEK	TITLE	ARTIST	LABEL	WEEKS ON BOSS 30
(1)	1.	THE DOCK OF THE BAY	Otis Redding	Volt	6
(3)	2.	(THEME FROM) VALLEY OF THE DOLLS	Dionne Warwick	Scepter	6
(5)	3.	I THANK YOU	Sam & Dave	Stax	5
(6)	4.	WORDS	The Bee Gees	Atco	5
(11)	5.	I'M GONNA MAKE YOU LOVE ME	Madeline Bell	Philips	4
(23)	6.	THE MIGHTY QUINN	Manfred Mann	Mercury	2
(18)	7.	KISS ME GOODBYE	Petula Clark	Warner Bros.	3
(17)	8.	THE END OF OUR ROAD	Gladys Knight & The Pips	Soul	4
(20)	9.	LA-LA-MEANS I LOVE YOU	The Delfonics	Philly Groove	3
(22)	10.	MISSION: IMPOSSIBLE	Lalo Schifrin	Dot	3
(21)	11.	EVERYTHING THAT TOUCHES YOU	The Association	Warner Bros.	5
(2)	12.	JUST DROPPED IN To See What Condition My Condition Was In	The First Edition	Reprise	5
(29)	13.	ME ABOUT YOU	Jackie De Shannon	Imperial	2
(10)	14.	I WISH IT WOULD RAIN	The Temptations	Gordy	7
(28)	15.	SINCE YOU'VE BEEN GONE	Aretha Franklin	Atlantic	2
(8)	16.	LOOK, HERE COMES THE SUN	The Sunshine Company	Imperial	6
(7)	17.	SIMON SAYS	1910 Fruitgum Co.	Buddah	4
(4)	18.	LOVE IS BLUE	Paul Mauriat	Philips	8
(9)	19.	SUMMERTIME BLUES	Blue Cheer	Philips	3
(25)	20.	COUNTRY GIRL—CITY MAN	Billy Vera & Judy Clay	Atlantic	3
(26)	21.	SOUL COAXING	Raymond Lefevre	4 Corners of The World	2
(15)	22.	BOTTLE OF WINE	The Fireballs	Atco	3
(16)	23.	WE'RE A WINNER	The Impressions	ABC	6
(30)	24.	WILL YOU LOVE ME TOMORROW	The 4 Seasons	Philips	2
(HB)	25.	SCARBOROUGH FAIR	Simon & Garfunkel	Columbia	1
(27)	26.	DANCE TO THE MUSIC	Sly & The Family Stone	Epic	2
(HB)	27.	THE BALLAD OF BONNIE AND CLYDE	Georgie Fame	Epic	1
(HB)	28.	CAB DRIVER	The Mills Brothers	Dot	1
(HB)	29.	YOUNG GIRL	The Union Gap	Columbia	1
(HB)	30.	MEN ARE GETTIN' SCARCE	Joe Tex	Dial	1

OFFICIAL ISSUE NO. 139

The popularity of records listed herein is the opinion of KHJ based on its survey of record sales in Southern California correlated with listener requests.

Radio has its first billion-dollar year, with gross sales up 12% over the previous year, and radio ad sales are at their highest in 10 years.

Billboard magazine names **"The Real" Don Steele** the No. 1 air personality in influencing the sales of record singles. Steele, born Donald S. Revert in Hollywood, California on April 1, 1936, is one of the most popular disc jockeys in the United States, gaining fame on radio station KHJ-AM Los Angeles, where he promotes the top-40 "Boss" radio format.

1968 ADVERTISEMENT

Popular Music

A Harder Edge

By 1968, some appear cynically ready to write off the peace and love generation, which raised its freak flag at 1967's historic Monterey Pop Festival, going so far as to stage a mock funeral for a San Francisco hippie effigy following the crashing end to the Summer of Love. A nascent trend in rock 'n roll finds the music inching off its blues-folk base toward a harder-edged sound, though some of the godfathers of the swelling heavy metal movement hedge their bets. The hard blues power trio **Cream**, having had enough of the high-decibel concert circuit, call it quits, while **Jimi Hendrix**—weary of guitar stunts and anxious to strut his real stuff—opts for a more complex approach on the ambitious jazz-tinged LP *Electric Ladyland.* Nevertheless, many are poised to pick up the power chord gauntlet.

Things get heavy on California's West Coast, as the band **Steppenwolf** releases its self-titled debut album, including what might well be considered a metal anthem—the driving hit "Born to Be Wild." The song also supplies a name for the genre via its "heavy-metal thunder" lyric. More leaden still, **Iron Butterfly** offers up the LP *In-A-Gadda-Da-Vida*, whose thumping 17-minute title track has a long drum solo embedded within. Even Butterfly's members seem at a loss to explain the song's title, its origin lost in a fog.

Across the pond, the fertile ground laid by the bluesy **Yardbirds** yields the **Jeff Beck Group**. Guitarist Beck's band includes singer **Rod Stewart** plus future **Rolling Stone Ron Wood**. Their album *Truth* lists "I Ain't Superstitious" among its tracks. Another Yardbird electric guitar alumnus, **Jimmy Page**, forms **Led Zeppelin**, featuring **Robert Plant**'s unearthly vocal wailings. Yet to release their first album with its quaking hit "Whole Lotta Love," the group nevertheless establishes itself as a formidable live entity in anticipation of their reputation as the greatest of all metal bands. Dervish/flautist **Ian Anderson** fronts **Jethro Tull**, whose LP *This Was* foreshadows their unique brand of English agrarian metal. Also of note: **Deep Purple**, whose *Shades of Deep Purple* produces the hit "Hush."

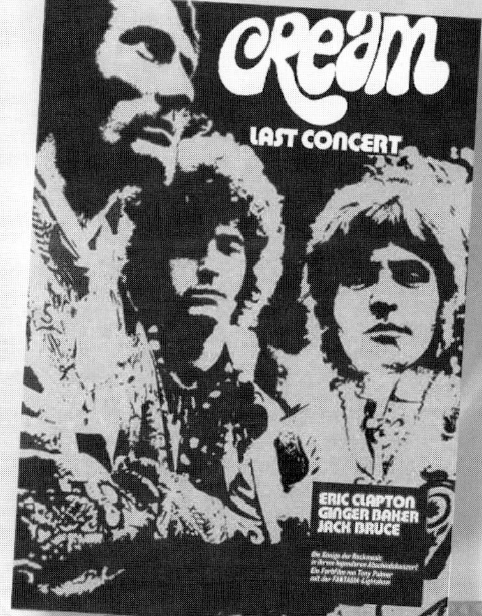

Cream, *l to r: Ginger Baker, Eric Clapton, Jack Bruce*

Steppenwolf, *below l to r: Goldy McJohn, Rushton Moreve, Jerry Edmonton, Mike Monarch, John Kay*

Iron Butterfly, *below l to r: Doug Ingle, Lee Dorman, Ron Bushy, Erik Brann*

Jeff Beck Group, *above right l to r: Aynsley Dunbar, Jeff Beck, Rod Stewart, Ron Wood*

Jethro Tull, *right l to r: Glenn Cornick, Ian Anderson, Clive Bunker, Martin Barre*

Led Zeppelin, *below l to r: John Bonham, Robert Plant, Jimmy Page, John Paul Jones*

BeatlesJournal

THE BEATLES, their significant others, and assorted celebrities descend en masse on India's **Maharishi Mahesh Yogi** to get their om on and find out firsthand what all the transcendental meditation fuss is about. Some are less enchanted than **George Harrison**, who is already a student of Indian music and an acolyte of all things spiritual. In particular, **John Lennon** expresses his disenchantment with the Maharishi and departs early.

Some of those sentiments find their way into compositions on the Beatles' ninth album—a two-disk extravaganza titled "The Beatles," but better known as the White Album. The song "Sexy Sadie" is a thinly veiled dressing-down of the Maharishi, while "Dear Prudence" refers to actress **Mia Farrow**'s sister, who stays locked away in her room for the duration of the Indian encampment.

There is a good deal of discord during the recording of the White Album, with **Ringo Starr** in particular feeling under-appreciated. All turns out well, however, and the production yields a wealth of Beatle treasures in addition to becoming their all-time best-seller.

While the Beatles record the White Album, they simultaneously launch their multifaceted Apple Corps company, whose Apple Records label will issue all future Beatles-related material as well as a number of other artists who sign on. The enterprise will prove to be only intermittently successful, with Beatles product being the sole profit earner. The company will also tussle repeatedly with Apple Computer, Inc. regarding domain over the Apple symbol and name.

Meanwhile, **John Lennon** and wife **Yoko Ono** court controversy with their "Two Virgins" LP release, an avant-garde experiment featuring the twosome nude on the front and back covers. Police confiscate copies of the record and one music store is actually shut down. "Two Virgins" subsequently ships in a brown paper wrapper imprinted with a Bible verse.

Left: Beatles and others in India. Above: Two Virgins *front and back. Right: The White Album package with photos and poster.*

SOME IMPORTANT ALBUMS

Music From Big Pink is the debut album from **The Band**. The group's moniker springs from their tenure as Bob Dylan's backup group, and his presence is felt on *Pink* via several of his compositions including "I Shall Be Released." Robbie Robertson's classic "The Weight" is here as well.

Bookends, the 5th from **Simon and Garfunkel**, catapults to the top of *Billboard*'s album list thanks in part to the popularity of the film *The Graduate* and its soundtrack. The LP includes the chart-topping "Mrs. Robinson," as well as "A Hazy Shade of Winter," "At the Zoo," and the plaintive "America." One of the best collections to spring from the pen of Paul Simon.

The Natch'l Blues from **Taj Mahal** goes a long way toward reminding rock and pop fans of the debt they owe to the music's roots. Singer/guitarist Taj bridges the gap by adding his funky, propulsive kick to traditional material, making it instantly relevant to the uninitiated.

Jim Morrison and **The Doors** score their first #1 LP with ***Waiting for the Sun***, which includes the monster single "Hello, I Love You." The album marks a slight retreat from the band's adventurous and provocative ways, but includes strong songs like "Love Street" and "Five to One."

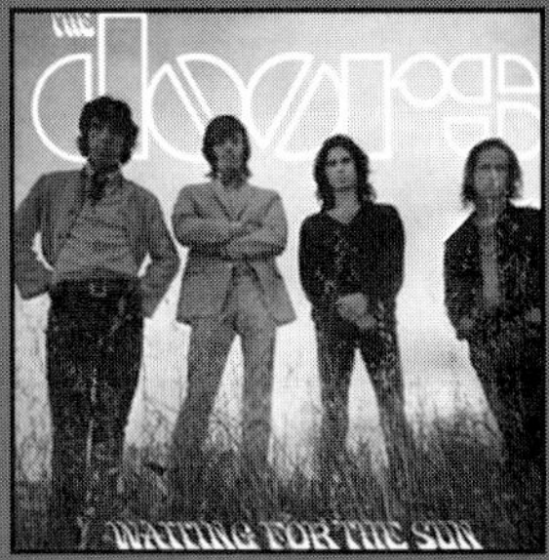

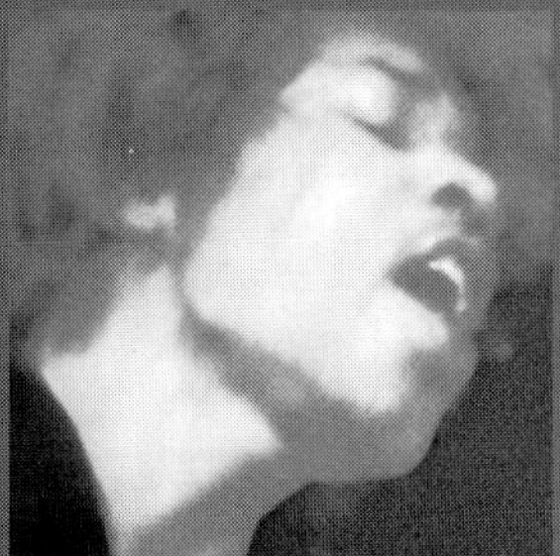

The two-disk ***Electric Ladyland***, the final studio album from **Jimi Hendrix,** is his magnum opus. Filled with gypsy guitars and haunting refrains, it is a record for the ages that reveals itself slowly to the listener. Included is Hendrix' rendition of Dylan's "All Along the Watchtower," which may be the definitive version.

Beggars Banquet marks the final recording of guitarist Brian Jones with the **Rolling Stones**. One of their best efforts, the LP is notable for its rootsy slide guitar and mandolin touches, as well as it's inclusion of Stones anthems "Sympathy for the Devil" and "Street Fighting Man."

Buffalo Springfield doesn't so much break up as disintegrate under the strain of the kinds of problems that typically plague rock groups. ***Last Time Around*** is memorable as the swan song of a good band whose members go on to define rock music for years to come, including Neil Young and Stephen Stills. "Kind Woman" and "I am a Child" are standout tracks.

The progressive, jazzy rock of **Traffic** unfolds on their eponymous 2nd album. Steve Winwood, Jim Capaldi and Chris Wood welcome Dave Mason back to their lineup, though he has a limited presence. Some of the British group's signature songs are here, including "Feelin' Alright" and "40,000 Headmen."

Not a great commercial success, **Van Morrison**'s impressionistic ***Astral Weeks*** enjoys critical acclaim and grows gradually in public estimation. Unusual and adventurous, it is another step toward solidifying Morrison's reputation as perhaps the best white R&B singer.

Tiny Tim is easy to write off as a stringy-haired warbling joke—a reputation he does nothing to discourage. But the ukulele-strummer is a musicologist who knows his stuff and ***God Bless Tiny Tim*** has many tuneful pleasures to offer, plus "Tip-Toe Through the Tulips," if you must have it.

Tammi Terrell and Marvin Gaye

It Takes Two

Singer/writer/multi-instrumentalist **Marvin Gaye** is already a prolific hitmaker for Motown Records when he embarks on a series of duet recordings with female singers, including **Mary Wells** and **Kim Weston**. But it is his pairing with **Tammi Terrell** that produces heat as well as sparks, as evidenced by 1967's *United* LP, which yields the smash "Ain't No Mountain High Enough." After Tammi collapses in Gaye's arms during a concert performance—later to be diagnosed with a fatal brain tumor—he spirals into depression. Motown continues to release the fruits of the Gaye-Terrell pairing, and "Ain't Nothing Like The Real Thing" and "You're All I Need To Get By" are big hits. Then, proving that you can't keep a good man down, Gaye goes on to record the biggest hit of his career—the #1 "I Heard It Through the Grapevine."

It would be difficult to name a blues artist who has a bigger impact on the era's rock stars than the great guitarist, singer and composer **Muddy Waters**, hailing from Chicago by way of Mississippi. Since such guitarists as **Eric Clapton** and **Jimmy Page** have received so much from him, no one can blame Muddy for turning the tables and recording an album like *Electric Mud.* Blues purists cringe at the psychedelic renderings of Muddy classics like "Mannish Boy" and "I'm Your Hoochie Coochie Man," and even the artist himself puts the LP down, calling it "not real blues." But it makes a lot of money for him and comes to be regarded as an influential album by many future rock and even hip-hop talents.

Muddy Waters

Soul music is dealt a body blow by the assassination of **Martin Luther King, Jr.**, and faces the future with uncertainty. **Stax** Records scrambles to revive their recording roster while reeling from the loss of their biggest artist, **Otis Redding**, who died in a tragic 1967 plane crash. The label signs the veteran **Staple Singers** while **Isaac Hayes** shows promise with his second LP, *Hot Buttered Soul.*

Sly Stone

The Motown hit machine sputters as well, though the reliable **Diana Ross and the Supremes** deliver the hit "Love Child." **Stevie Wonder** and the **Isley Brothers** also have a good year.

Aretha Franklin

Elsewhere, the rock-funk combination of **Sly and the Family Stone** produces the Top 10 hit "Dance to the Music," while **James Brown** scores a signature hit with "Say It Loud-I'm Black and I'm Proud" and **Aretha Franklin** has a chart-topper in "Think."

Diana Ross (top) and the Supremes

Jazz

Wes Montgomery, *often considered the greatest of post-bop jazz guitarists, dies of a heart attack at age 45.*

The 2nd annual **Montreux Jazz Festival** is held from June 12 to 16. The Bill Evans Trio tops the bill and Nina Simone performs one of her first concerts.

In the U.S., the 15th annual **Newport Jazz Festival** attracts record crowds.

Veteran producer **Creed Taylor**'s CTI Records is the most vital new label in jazz. Characterized by lush orchestrations and striking gatefold album covers, CTI's roster includes **Wes Montgomery**, **Herbie Mann**, **Antonio Carlos Jobim**, **Paul Desmond**, and new guitar phenomenon and Wes Montgomery heir apparent, **George Benson**.

Duke Ellington, age 70, receives the Congressional Medal of Freedom at the White House on his birthday.

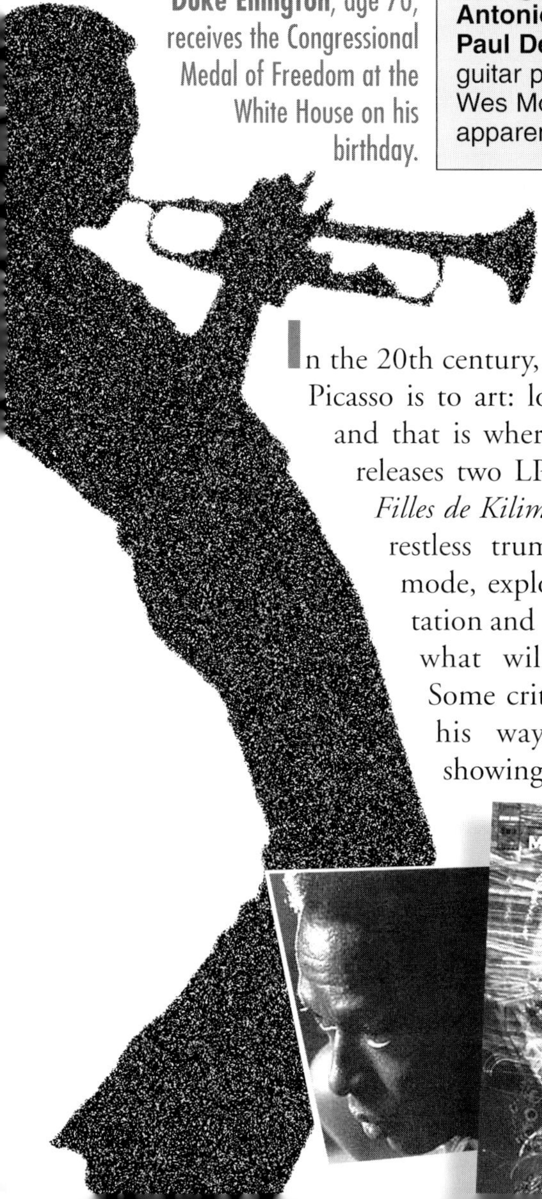

MILES AHEAD

In the 20th century, **Miles Davis** is to jazz as Picasso is to art: look for the cutting edge and that is where you'll find him. Miles releases two LPs—*Miles in the Sky* and *Filles de Kilimanjaro.* They present the restless trumpeter in a transitional mode, exploring electric instrumentation and laying the foundation for what will become jazz fusion. Some critics think Miles is losing his way; others insist he is showing the way.

down beat Critics Poll

Hall of Fame Sidney Bechet/Fats Waller
Jazz Album of the Year Duke Ellington *Far East Suite*
Big Band Duke Ellington
Acoustic Jazz Group Miles Davis
Alto Saxophone Johnny Hodges
Tenor Saxophone Sonny Rollins
Baritone Saxophone Harry Carney
Trumpet Miles Davis
Trombone J.J. Johnson
Clarinet Pee Wee Russell
Drums Elvin Jones
Vibes Milt Jackson
Acoustic Bass Richard Davis
Guitar Kenny Burrell
Piano Bill Evans
Organ Jimmy Smith
Miscellaneous Instrument Jean-Luc Ponty-Violin
Arranger Duke Ellington
Composer Duke Ellington
Male Vocalist Louis Armstrong/Ray Charles
Female Vocalist Ella Fitzgerald

Duke Ellington

Left to right: Dionne Warwick, Burt Bacharach, Herb Alpert, Sérgio Mendes

Composer **Burt Bacharach** and lyricist **Hal David** continue their winning streak, with a number of artists enjoying chart success on the strength of their irresistible pop confections. The team tackles a musical, *Promises, Promises,* which yields several top tunes, including "I'll Never Fall in Love Again" and the title number—a hit for **Dionne Warwick** hot on the heels of 1967's "I Say a Little Prayer." Warwick scores yet again with Bacharach's "Do You Know the Way to San Jose."

Although trumpet player **Herb Alpert** and his **Tijuana Brass** outsell all other musical artists in the '60s, save the **Beatles**, **Elvis**, and **Sinatra**, a #1 hit eludes him. But a rare solo vocal effort on a TV special—never intended for record release—generates such demand that Bacharach's "This Guy's In Love With You" finally rockets Alpert to the top spot. **Sérgio Mendes & Brasil '66**, who record for Alpert's A&M records, also strike gold with "The Look of Love," a Bacharach song from the Academy Award-winning soundtrack of the movie *Casino Royale*.

BORN IN 1968 ★

TONI BRAXTON

KENNY CHESNEY

ZIGGY MARLEY

SARAH McLACHLAN

CARNIE WILSON

THOM YORKE

(pictured)

The music world says goodbye to:

Country Music Hall of Fame singer **RED FOLEY** (58) dies of a heart attack. Foley sold over 25 million records including "Peace in the Valley" and "One By One."

Red Foley

Guitarist **LUTHER PERKINS** (40) succumbs to injuries sustained in a home fire. He was a mainstay of Johnny Cash's band, renowned for his "boom-chicka-boom" style of playing.

MARION WALTER "LITTLE WALTER" JACOBS (37) is generally regarded as the foremost blues harmonica player. His virtuosity and innovation continue to influence every musician who picks up the instrument. Little Walter's amplified sound can be heard to good effect on several R&B hits, including "Juke," and he is featured on many of Muddy Waters' best recordings. Injuries sustained in a fight cause his premature death.

Little Walter

COUNTRY & WESTERN

Singer and guitarist extraordinaire **GLEN CAMPBELL** is on a roll, following up last year's smash "Gentle on My Mind" with two Top 10 hits, including the plaintive "Wichita Lineman," destined to become one of his signature songs.

Tammy's Turn

Tammy Wynette has a way of connecting with people, especially women. Maybe it's the hard life she's led, by turns waitress, barmaid, and factory worker—all while caring for a sick child. She's real, and she doesn't quit. Knocking on doors and pounding the pavement finally pays off for the singer. Three massive hit singles in one year help her lay claim to the title "First Lady of Country Music." "Take Me to Your World," "D-I-V-O-R-C-E," and "Stand by Your Man"— the song which will become her anthem— tell her story and the stories of American women everywhere.

The Country Music Association Awards are broadcast on television for the first time. Hosted by **Roy Rogers** and **Dale Evans**, the awards show is taped in October and aired on NBC a month later.

Captive Audience

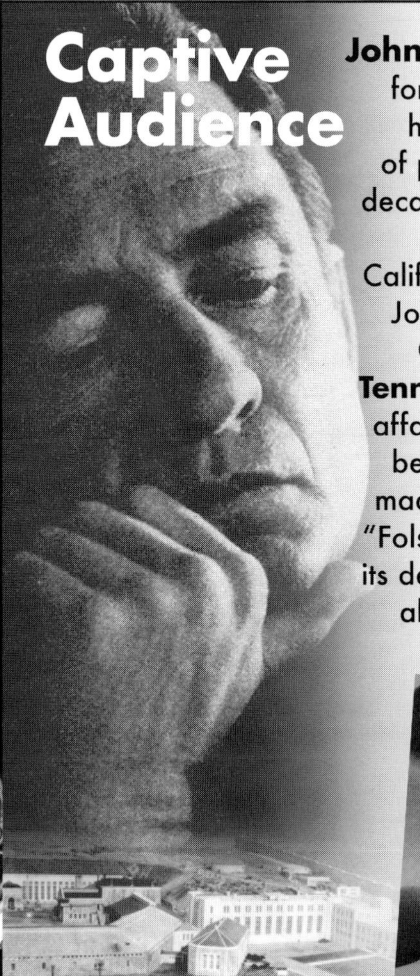

Johnny Cash's sympathy for the incarcerated had him performing in front of prison audiences for a decade before deciding to tape a live album at California's Folsom Prison. Joined by **June Carter**, **Carl Perkins** and the **Tennessee 3**, the raucous affair results in one of the best live recordings ever made, and Johnny's song "Folsom Prison Blues" gets its definitive treatment. The album is a smash hit for the "Man in Black."

No. 1 Country HITS

Sing Me Back Home	**Merle Haggard**
Skip a Rope	**Henson Cargill**
Take Me to Your World	**Tammy Wynette**
A World of Our Own	**Sonny James**
How Long Will My Baby Be Gone	**Buck Owens**
You Are My Treasure	**Jack Greene**
Fist City	**Loretta Lynn**
The Legend of Bonnie and Clyde	**Merle Haggard**
Have a Little Faith	**David Houston**
I Wanna Live	**Glen Campbell**
Honey	**Bobby Goldsboro**
D-I-V-O-R-C-E	**Tammy Wynette**
Folsom Prison Blues	**Johnny Cash**
Heaven Says Hello	**Sonny James**
Already It's Heaven	**David Houston**
Mama Tried	**Merle Haggard**
Harper Valley P.T.A.	**Jeannie C. Riley**
Then You Can Tell Me Goodbye	**Eddy Arnold**
Next In Line	**Conway Twitty**
I Walk Alone	**Marty Robbins**
Stand by Your Man	**Tammy Wynette**
Born to Be With You	**Sonny James**
Wichita Lineman	**Glen Campbell**

Loretta Lynn

GRAMMY awards

Bill Cosby

Record of the Year
MRS. ROBINSON
Simon & Garfunkel

Song of the Year
LITTLE GREEN APPLES
Bobby Russell, writer

Album of the Year
BY THE TIME I GET TO PHOENIX
Glen Campbell

Vocal Performance, Female
DO YOU KNOW THE WAY TO SAN JOSE
Dionne Warwick

Vocal Performance, Male
LIGHT MY FIRE
José Feliciano

New Artist
JOSÉ FELICIANO

Rhythm & Blues Song
(SITTIN' ON) THE DOCK OF THE BAY
Otis Redding / Steve Cropper, writers

Rhythm & Blues Vocal, Female
CHAIN OF FOOLS
Aretha Franklin

Rhythm & Blues Vocal, Male
(SITTIN' ON) THE DOCK OF THE BAY
Otis Redding

Rhythm & Blues Group, Vocal or Instrumental
CLOUD NINE
The Temptations

Jazz Performance, Small Group
LIVE AT MONTREUX
Bill Evans Trio

Jazz Performance, Large Group
AND HIS MOTHER CALLED HIM BILL
Duke Ellington

Country Vocal, Female
HARPER VALLEY P.T.A.
Jeannie C. Riley

Country Vocal, Male
FOLSOM PRISON BLUES
Johnny Cash

Folk Performance
BOTH SIDES NOW
Judy Collins

Best Opera Recording
Mozart, Cosi Fan Tutti
Leontyne Price, et al
New Philharmonia Orchestra

Classical Performance, Orchestra
Debussy, La Mer, Jeux
Pierre Boulez
New Philharmonia Orchestra

Comedy Performance
TO RUSSELL, MY BROTHER
Bill Cosby

Judy Collins

Bill Evans

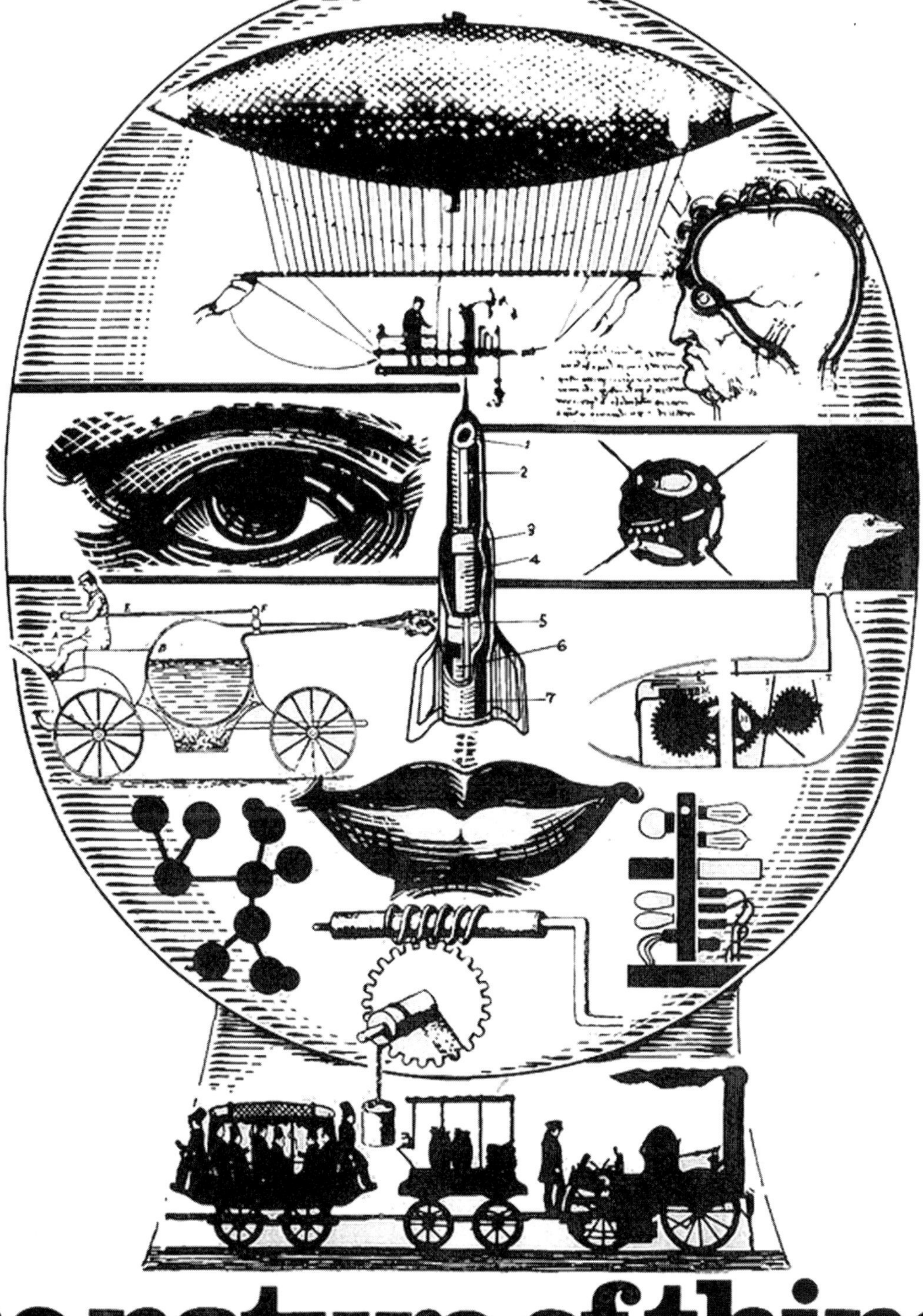

the nature of things

Can computers actually think?
How does color television work?
What makes a clock tick?
How do airplanes fly?
In an informative entertaining way,
The Nature of Things looks at machines,
how they are affecting our lives today,
and what's in store for the future.

CBC

**10:30 P.M.
THURSDAYS**

Classical Music

S*WITCHED-ON BACH*, an album of selections from **Johann Sebastian Bach** performed by **Wendy Carlos** on a Moog synthesizer, quickly achieves platinum sales status. It eclipses all previous classical records in terms of sales, stays in *Billboard*'s Top 10 for 17 weeks, and will go on to win multiple Grammy Awards and create great interest in electronic music in general and Moog synthesizers in particular.

Another electronic music pioneer, Italian composer **Luciano Berio**, premieres his *Sinfonia,* which incorporates *O King*—music dedicated to the late Martin Luther King, Jr.

Elsewhere in the avant-garde, minimalist composer **Terry Riley**'s 1964 composition *In C* is recorded, and **George Crumb**, winner of the Pulitzer Prize for music, unveils *Songs, Drones, and Refrains of Death.*

David Tudor and **Lowell Cross** premiere *Reunion*, performed in conjunction with a chess game that triggers lighting effects. At the piece's debut, **John Cage** (r) and artist **Marcel Duchamp** engage in the match.

NOTABLE NEW LPs

Hector Berlioz:
REQUIEM
Charles Münch
Orchester des Bayerischen and Chorus
(Münch dies while touring with Orchestre de Paris.)

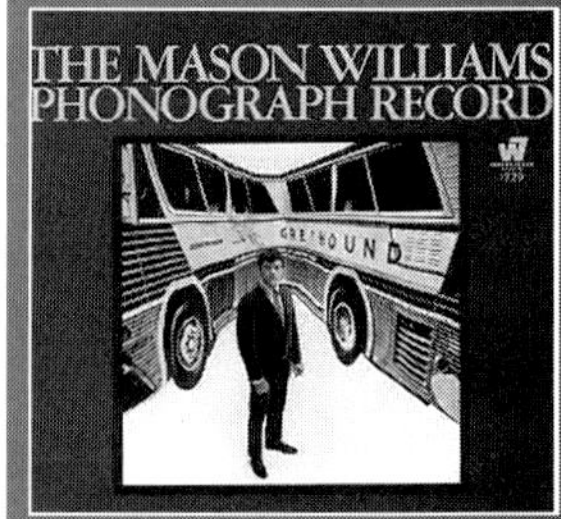

THE MASON WILLIAMS PHONOGRAPH RECORD
Mason Williams
(Not a classical record, strictly speaking, but contains the Grammy-winning "Classical Gas.")

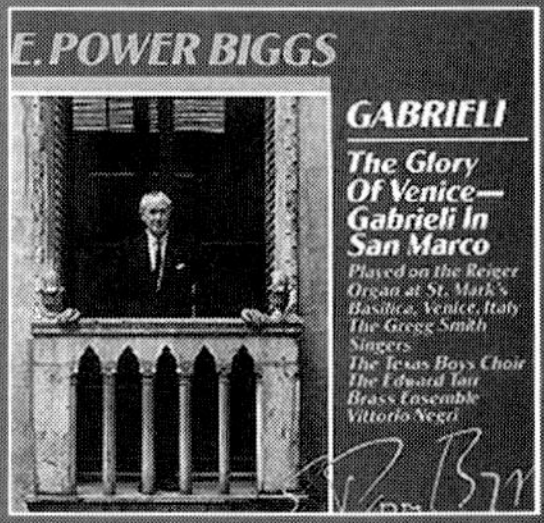

Gabrieli:
THE GLORY OF VENICE—GABRIELI IN SAN MARCO
E. Power Biggs & The Gregg Smith Singers

POP MUSIC Inspired by the **CLASSICS**

"Emerald City" by **The Seekers** is based on **Beethoven**'s "Ode to Joy" from his *Ninth Symphony.*

"Hall of the Mountain King" by **The Who** is based on **Edvard Grieg**'s *Peer Gynt Suite.*

"Prelude B - I'm So Glad" by **Deep Purple** is inspired by **Rimsky-Korsakov**'s *Scheherazade: The Sea and Sinbad's Ship.*

"All You Need is Love" by **The Beatles** contains a small piece from **J.S. Bach**'s *2-part Invention no. 8.*

"Fur Elise/Moonlight Sonata" by **Vanilla Fudge** is based on **Beethoven**'s bagatelle *Für Elise* and *Piano Sonata no. 14, Moonlight.*

Bernstein

As **Leonard Bernstein** becomes laureate conductor of the New York Philharmonic at the close of the 1968-69 season, fall concerts begin with **George Szell** serving as chief artistic overseer while continuing as music director of the Cleveland Orchestra. The New York Philharmonic spends late summer touring Israel and nine European countries.

The Cincinnati Symphony announces that it will visit Europe in the spring of 1969, celebrating its 75th season.

Previn

André Previn becomes the 10th principal conductor of the London Symphony while remaining music director of the Houston Symphony.

Henry Lewis becomes the first African American ever to be named music director of a leading American orchestra when he takes his position with the New Jersey Symphony.

The Cleveland Orchestra takes possession of Blossom Music Center in Cuyahoga Falls, Ohio, about 30 miles south of Cleveland.

Atlanta dedicates Symphony Hall in October, and the Seattle Symphony opens its 65th season.

Opera News

- The Metropolitan Opera of New York sustains a $3.5 million annual operating loss.
- The Santa Fe, New Mexico Opera, which lost its theater to fire the previous year, returns with a beautiful new outdoor opera house.
- The Lyric Opera of Chicago, which lost its 1967 season to a labor dispute, resumes production.
- The Lincoln Center Festival brings the Rome Opera to New York.
- The St. Louis Municipal Opera marks its 50th year.
- Built in 1904, the London Coliseum reopens as home to the English National Opera Company.

London Coliseum

Construction of phase 2 of the Sydney, Australia Opera House—the outer shells—nears completion. Planning for the massive project began in the late 1940s.

Isn't that Terence Stamp behind those Foster Grants?

(Good guess. Catch him as "Blue". A Paramount picture.)

As Mr. Stamp and the tuned-in world have discovered, there's more to sunglasses than meets the eye. Slip into a pair and something inside seems to click. A heightened self-awareness. A subtle increase of confidence. Of coolth.

These pictures, taken recently on villa-laden Appia Antica outside Rome, reveal just how our latest Foster Grants wrought their magic on Terence.

That's why they're called the Sunglasses of the Stars.

Sunglasses have become fun glasses. And everybody, everywhere, is wearing them.

Foster Grant, #1 in the anti-glare crusade, is tickled pink. We make more shades in more styles and more colors than anybody. Anywhere. All with ff77 lenses that pass the most rigid U.S. Gov't standards for eye protection (standards a lot of those expensive imports flunk). All with down-to-earth price tags.

Pick up a pair of Foster Grants next time you're downtown. If they're moving, smile.

It may be someone you know.

"Actually I quite fancy you, Your Highness. It's your type I detest."

"I'm afraid that would mean a swim, dear lady. My bumbling lackeys have already raised the drawbridge."

"Now what's this I hear, Fingers, about withholding the Vegas receipts from the bosom of your family?"

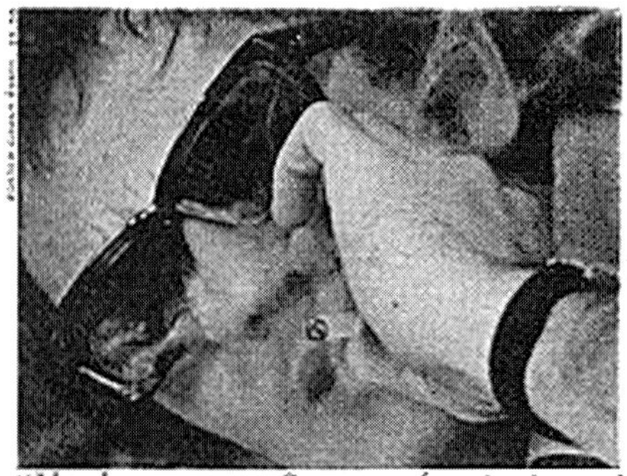

"You have a way, Senator, of saying 'peace' as if it were a dirty word."

"The Peace Corps? Haight-Ashbury? Mecca? Decisions, decisions, decisions."

"You just tell her Che Guevara's here and would like a word with

Dance

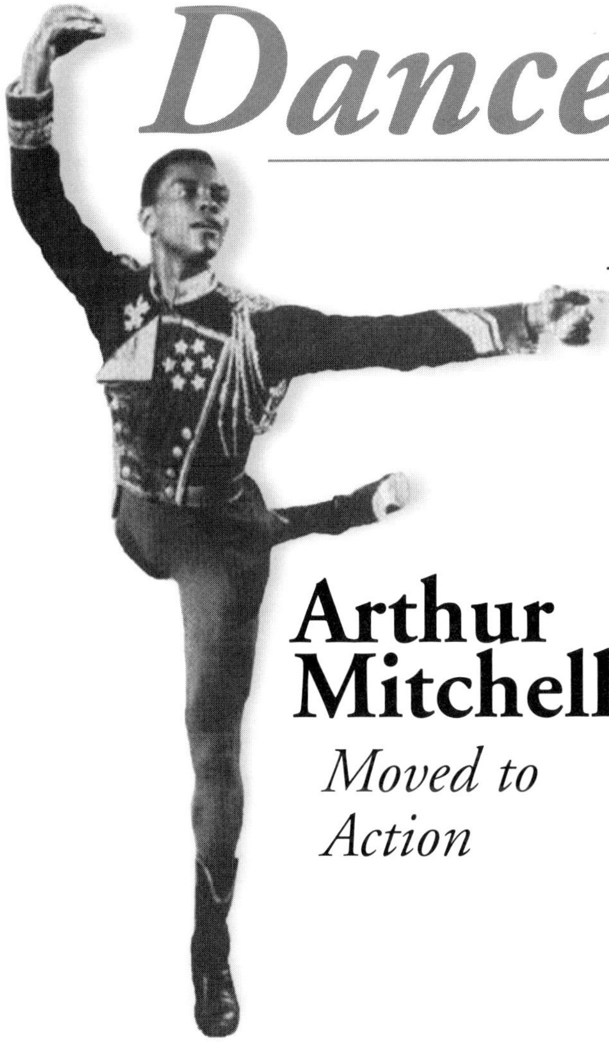

Arthur Mitchell

Moved to Action

African American choreographer and dancer **ARTHUR MITCHELL** has a driving desire to prove that ballet need not be an exclusively white domain. On learning of the assassination of **Dr. Martin Luther King, Jr.**, the **George Balanchine** protégé and principal dancer with the New York City Ballet determines to open a dance school in Harlem. Setting up in a garage, he starts with 30 kids and two dancers. In four months he has 400 students. His fledgling enterprise will quickly become the Dance Theatre of Harlem.

Mitchell also performs on television's *Tonight Show*, raising eyebrows and breaking barriers by partnering with a white female dancer.

Capping a busy year, Mitchell premieres his new piece, *Rhythmetron.*

Eleo Pomare, Rod Rodgers, and others form the Association of Black Choreographers.

The Harlem Cultural Commission launches "Dancemobile," taking performers like Pomare, Rodgers, and others to the streets on a flatbed truck during the city's long, hot summers.

CAPEZIO AWARD

Lucia Chase
founder and director of American Ballet Theatre

Early modern dance pioneer and Martha Graham teacher **Ruth St. Denis** dies at age 91.

The New York City Ballet performs at the New York State Theater in Lincoln Center and premieres choreographer **George Balanchine**'s *La Source.*

City Center Joffrey Ballet performs at the New York City Center, presenting **Gerald Arpino**'s *The Clowns* for the first time.

The American Ballet Theatre is the first American company to perform at the Metropolitan Opera House, and becomes the official ballet company of the Kennedy Center for the Performing Arts in Washington, D.C.

In August, the Ford Foundation grants $485,000 to three New York City theaters for presentation of modern dance. At the same time, the New York State Council on the Arts awards grants to the Brooklyn Academy of Music and the State University of New York.

Balanchine

1968 ADVERTISEMENT

Put your family album on TV.

Instead of watching the stars hamming it up on TV, you can also watch your family hamming it up on TV. Sylvania has invented an amazing machine called the Scanner Color Slide Theatre. It gives you color TV, color slides, and a cassette tape recorder all in one cabinet.

Sounds like magic. But there's really no hokus-pokus involved. Sylvania's three-in-oner has a built-in slide system that electronically transmits your regular home slides on to your TV screen. Without dragging out a slide projector. Without setting up a screen. And without rearranging furniture. You can go from TV to slides as easy as changing a channel.

You can make your slides "talkies" if you prerecord your voice on the built-in cassette tape recorder. That way you don't have to go through the same travelogue over and over again. You just show your slides and your recorded voice comes out automatically synchronized with the pictures. Or you can really go Hollywood and tape a sound track of swashbuckling background music to liven up your "Man-defying-Nature" camping trips at Beaver Dam Lake.

If a shot is too light, darken it. If it's too dark, lighten it. It's as easy as adjusting color on a TV set.

And oh what color! The reproduction you get is only from the world's best all-around color TV set. But don't take our word for it. If you feel seeing is believing, drop in to a Sylvania dealer. And bring your family album along. For a screen test.

SYLVANIA
A SUBSIDIARY OF GENERAL TELEPHONE & ELECTRONICS

Picture simulated

Sylvania's color TV that shows color slides.

For the address of your nearest Sylvania dealer make a free call to (800) 243-0355. In Connecticut call 853-3600.
For an illustrated brochure send 25c to Sylvania Entertainment Products, 1100 Main St., Buffalo, N.Y. 14209, Dept. L-1.

ON BROADWAY

SIMPLY SIMON

Former TV writer NEIL SIMON is Broadway's most reliable comedy playwright. He follows up his previous successes—*Barefoot in the Park, The Odd Couple,* and *Sweet Charity*—with the riotous *Plaza Suite*, which follows George C. Scott and Maureen Stapleton as a married couple attempting to rekindle their romance in New York's Plaza Hotel. One hit per year no longer being sufficient for the Emmy- and Tony-winning Mr. Simon, he enjoys additional success with the musical *Promises, Promises.*

Neil Simon (l), Maureen Stapleton, George C. Scott

new musicals

In 1924 Crete, a young student encounters island native **ZORBA**, whom he enlists to help him get a mining venture off the ground. The lusty Greek's appetites soon overwhelm the already shaky venture and the student is taught hard lessons in life and love, while Zorba learns a thing or two about responsibility—or not. **Herschel Bernardi** plays the title role, later made even more famous by **Anthony Quinn** in the film version, *Zorba the Greek.* **Maria Karnilova**, **Carmen Alvarez** and **John Cunningham** are also featured. Spirited dancing, stirring bouzouki music, ribaldry, and songs like "Life Is" and "I Am Free" ensure over 300 Broadway performances. Music by John Kander and lyrics by Fred Ebb.

An affirmation of the counterculture through a story involving drugs, Vietnam politics, flag desecration and hippies, much of it performed in the nude, **HAIR**—subtitled ***The American Tribal Love Rock-Musical***—creates a stir even in its initial performances at a New York go-go club called the Cheetah. Written by **James Rado** and **Gerome Ragni** (book and lyrics), and **Galt MacDermot** (music), *Hair* quickly moves to an off-Broadway location on its way to becoming a mainstream Broadway sensation. The show raises eyebrows, but the controversy over *Hair* may have amounted to little if not for a lot of very good songs, many of which subsequently hit the pop charts, including "Hair," "Where Do I Go?," "Easy to Be Hard," "Aquarius" and "Good Morning Starshine."

new musicals

Promises, Promises

It seems like composer **Burt Bacharach** is everywhere. Combining his Midas touch with playwright **Neil Simon**'s script—based on **Billy Wilder**'s hit film *The Apartment*—yields Broadway gold. **PROMISES, PROMISES,** about a philandering boss, a cowed employee, and a love nest used for clandestine amorous encounters, runs for 1,281 performances at the Shubert with **Jerry Orbach** as the hapless junior executive. As well, the song "I'll Never Fall in Love Again" provides a monster pop hit for singer **Dionne Warwick**.

Songwriter, dancer, producer, director—**George M. Cohan** was the heart and soul of the musical-comedy stage in the vaudeville era. **GEORGE M!** pays tribute to the grand old man in a musical biography. All of his flag-waving anthems are deftly woven into the story, including "Over There"—which embodies the patriotic spirit of World War I—"I'm a Yankee Doodle Dandy" and "You're a Grand Old Flag." The dynamic song-and-dance man **Joel Grey** has the title role, and the cast includes **Jerry Dodge**, **Jamie Donnelly** and **Bernadette Peters**.

SHOWS OPEN

Saint Joan

Exit the King

Before You Go

The Prime of Miss Jean Brodie

The Happy Time

I Never Sang for My Father

A Day in the Death of Joe Egg

The Price

Portrait of a Queen

Tiger at the Gates

The Guide

Weekend

Loot

The Cherry Orchard

Mike Downstairs

I'm Solomon

The Exercise

Cyrano de Bergerac

Soldiers

The Venetian Twins

Following her 6-week engagement at Broadway's Lunt-Fontanne Theatre, **MARLENE DIETRICH** moves to another extended stay at the Hellinger. The German-born actress/singer delves deeply into the repertoire of the songs, *lieder* and *chansons* she made famous as a cabaret performer and in her many Hollywood and European movies. Defying her 66 years, Dietrich looks fit and glamorous in a tight silver dress. The much-in-demand **Burt Bacharach** handles the arranging and conducting.

Comedian **Milton Berle** stars in the aptly named *The Goodbye People*, which closes after just 7 performances.

Woody Allen is rehearsing his comedy ***Play it Again, Sam,*** slated to open in early 1969.

Jane Alexander, center, and James Earl Jones, right

James Earl Jones has a career-defining role in *The Great White Hope*, a fictionalized account of the life of heavyweight boxer **Jack Johnson**. As boxer Jack Jefferson, Jones must deal with early-20th-century America's racial hatred of an outstanding black champion while he carries on a love affair with a white woman, played by **Jane Alexander**.

The Man in the Glass Booth, featuring **Harold Pinter**'s direction of a **Robert Shaw** play, centers on industrialist Arthur Goldman, a Jewish Holocaust survivor mistaken for a Nazi criminal and taken to Israel to stand trial. **Donald Pleasence** stars.

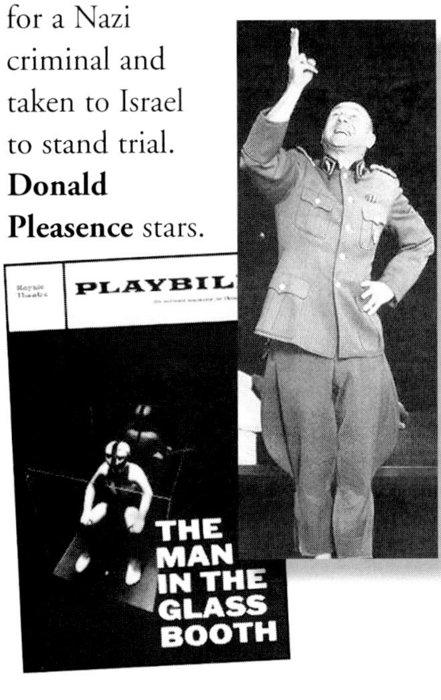

Albert Finney joins the cast of *A Day in the Death of Joe Egg*, a dark comedy about an English couple struggling to raise a disabled child.

SHOWS CLOSE

Hallelujah, Baby!

Illya Darling

The Birthday Party

The Little Foxes

Before You Go

Avanti!

Darling of the Day

Something Different

Staircase

More Stately Mansions

Weekend

Tiger at the Gates

Loot

Leda Had a Little Swan

Portrait of a Queen

Don't Drink the Water

Mike Downstairs

The Exercise

Soldiers

The Only Game in Town

New 125 cc!
Over 70 mph!
Under 175 lbs!
Over 70 mpg!
Under $400!
No matter how you put the numbers together, Rapido stacks up great. This is the new one from Harley-Davidson with a power-to-weight ratio that combines miles per hour with miles per gallon all day long. Rapido's quick acceleration and effortless top speed will startle you. The fine balance, big brakes and sure suspension will reassure you. So will the price tag. Dollar for dollar, there's nothing like Rapido on the road. Or on the track. Ride it. Compare it. Find out what plus-engineering is all about. Let Harley-Davidson put some fun ahead of you. Rapido 125. At the Harley-Davidson dealer near you.
N4655L
HARLEY-DAVIDSON
Harley-Davidson
priced to meet competition.
+ engineered to beat it.
Prices F.O.B. Warehouse.

TONY AWARDS

PLAY — ***Rosencrantz and Guildenstern Are Dead***
by Tom Stoppard

MUSICAL — ***Hallelujah, Baby!***
Book: Arthur Laurents
Music: Jule Styne
Lyrics: Betty Comden & Adolph Green

ACTOR/PLAY — **Martin Balsam**
You Know I Can't Hear You When the Water's Running

ACTRESS/PLAY — **Zoe Caldwell**
The Prime of Miss Jean Brodie

SUPPORTING ACTOR — **James Patterson**
The Birthday Party

SUPPORTING ACTRESS — **Zena Walker**
Joe Egg

ACTOR/MUSICAL — **Robert Goulet**
The Happy Time

ACTRESS/MUSICAL — **Patricia Routledge** (tie)
Darling of the Day
Leslie Uggams (tie)
Hallelujah, Baby!

DIRECTOR/PLAY — **Mike Nichols**
Plaza Suite

DIRECTOR/MUSICAL — **Gower Champion**
The Happy Time

Jack Benny and Carol Channing announce an award.

Tom Stoppard

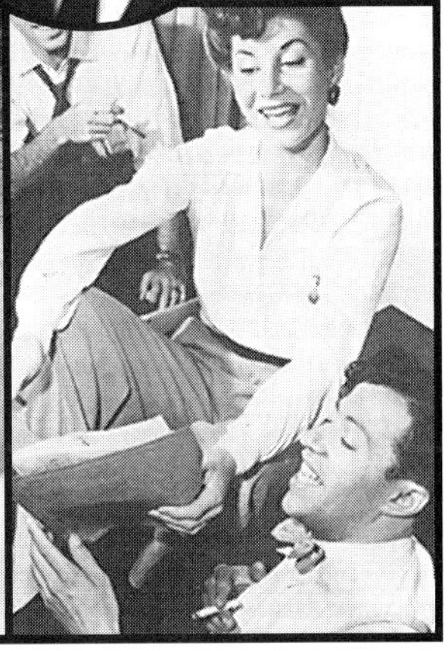

Jule Styne (l), Betty Comden and Adolph Green

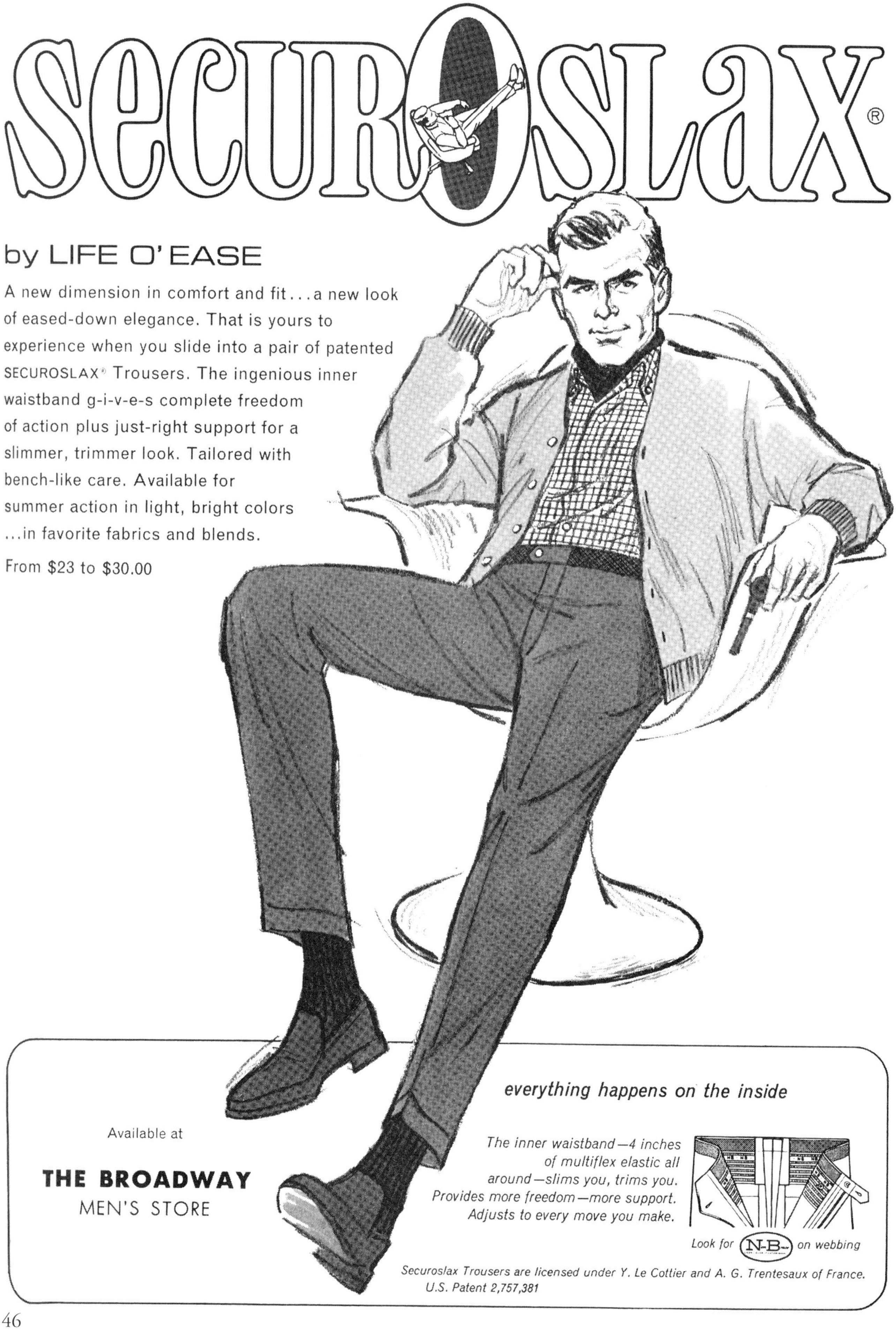
SECUROSLAX®
by LIFE O'EASE
A new dimension in comfort and fit . . . a new look of eased-down elegance. That is yours to experience when you slide into a pair of patented SECUROSLAX® Trousers. The ingenious inner waistband g-i-v-e-s complete freedom of action plus just-right support for a slimmer, trimmer look. Tailored with bench-like care. Available for summer action in light, bright colors . . . in favorite fabrics and blends.
From $23 to $30.00
everything happens on the inside
Available at
THE BROADWAY
MEN'S STORE
The inner waistband—4 inches of multiflex elastic all around—slims you, trims you. Provides more freedom—more support. Adjusts to every move you make.
Look for N-B on webbing
Securoslax Trousers are licensed under Y. Le Cottier and A. G. Trentesaux of France.
U.S. Patent 2,757,381

ART NEW TRENDS

Minimalist painters continue their quest to reduce painting to the essentials of geometric abstraction rendered with an extreme economy of means and color, **Sol LeWitt** and **Frank Stella** among them. Sculptors such as **Carl Andre** persist in making works that are flat or cubic and seamless, often hugging the floor or claiming the corner. The **Donald Judd** sculpture retrospective at the Whitney Museum of American Art goes a long way toward stamping the art establishment imprimatur on the movement. The leaning steel and lead works of **Richard Serra** begin to take on an imposing, even menacing monumentality.

Untitled *by Donald Judd*

One Ton Prop
by Richard Serra

Gyrostasis
by Robert Smithson

Inspired by the minimalist ethos and its use of elemental industrial materials like plywood and concrete, a new movement begins to emerge, variously known by the names Earth Art, Earthworks, or Land Art. The public gets its first glimpse via a group exhibition at New York's Dwan Gallery showing the works of **Robert Smithson**, **Walter De Maria**, **Michael Heizer**, and others. Though the initial modest gallery-bound works incorporate dirt, mud, sticks and mirrors, the movement's ultimate aim is to move art out of the gallery and away from civilization in the form of huge geologic displacements and landscape alteration on an often staggering scale. Earthworks raise questions about the nature of art, its place, and how it should be observed.

The Milwaukee, Wisconsin Art Center "Options in Art" exhibition is unique in that each piece can be manipulated by the viewer.

Kansas City's Nelson-Atkins Gallery features electronic works in its "Magic Theater" exhibition.

ANDY WARHOL *revisits his immensely popular Campbell's soup cans of the early '60s, adding "flavors" with a new series of screenprints.*

WHAT A YEAR IT WAS!

Bulgarian artist **Christo** and wife **Jeanne-Claude**, famous for wrapping buildings and other structures, participate in the Documenta 4 Art Fair in Kassel, Germany. They intend to build a package with a volume of 5,600 cubic meters – the largest inflated structure without a supporting skeleton ever created. After 3 failed attempts at raising the tethered gas-filled object, resulting in ruptures in the polyethylene skin, it is finally erected with help from a pair of the largest cranes in Europe.

New York artist **Chuck Close** is in the vanguard of Photorealist painting. His nearly 9-foot-tall monochrome *Big Self-Portrait* required 4 months to complete utilizing a grid system and airbrush, with paint so diluted that only a single tube of black is used for the piece.

New York's Museum of Modern Art mounts *Dada, Surrealism, and Their Heritage*. The works of the 1920s, '30s and '40s present a parallel to today's "destruction" art and to the new electronic and kinetic mediums.

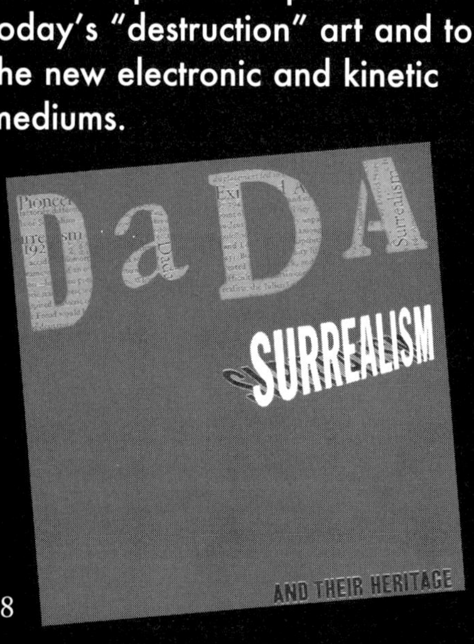

Dada artists photographed in 1922. From top, l to r: Paul Chadourne, Tristan Tzara, Philippe Soupault, Serge Charchoune, Man Ray (inset), Paul Eluard, Jacques Rigaut, Mick Soupault, Georges Ribemont-Dessaignes.

Many museums benefit from gifts this year. The Carnegie Institute Museum of Art in Pittsburgh, Pennsylvania receives one of **Van Gogh**'s last pictures from the Scaife Foundation, and the Museum of Modern Art in New York acquires the **Sidney and Harriet Janis** collection of modern art.

German-born American sculptor **Eva Hesse**, known for her unique work with latex, fiberglass, and plastics, holds her only one-person show of sculpture: *Chain Polymers* at the Fischbach Gallery in New York. She will die of a brain tumor in 1970.

The catalog for the Museum of Modern Art exhibit, *The Machine, As Seen at the End of the Mechanical Age*, has a stamped metal cover and hinges bound with rivets.

- PASSINGS -

Dutch painter **Kees van Dongen** (91) was known for his brightly colored erotic Fauve works.

French-born American citizen **Marcel Duchamp** (81) was one of the 20th century's most influential, mysterious, and interesting artists. Though affiliated with the Dada and Surrealist art movements, he remained fiercely independent, making his first big splash on the international art scene at the 1913 New York Armory Exhibition where he caused a scandal with his painting *Nude Descending a Staircase*, famously critcized as "an explosion in a shingle factory." He pioneered "ready-mades"—art created from appropriated items—and was renowned for his innovation, wit, and intellect.

Duchamp

Industrialist **Norton Simon** purchases the **Renoir** landscape *Le Pont des Arts* for $1,550,000. The painting will be displayed in California's nearly complete Pasadena Museum of Art, soon to be known as the Norton Simon Museum of Art.

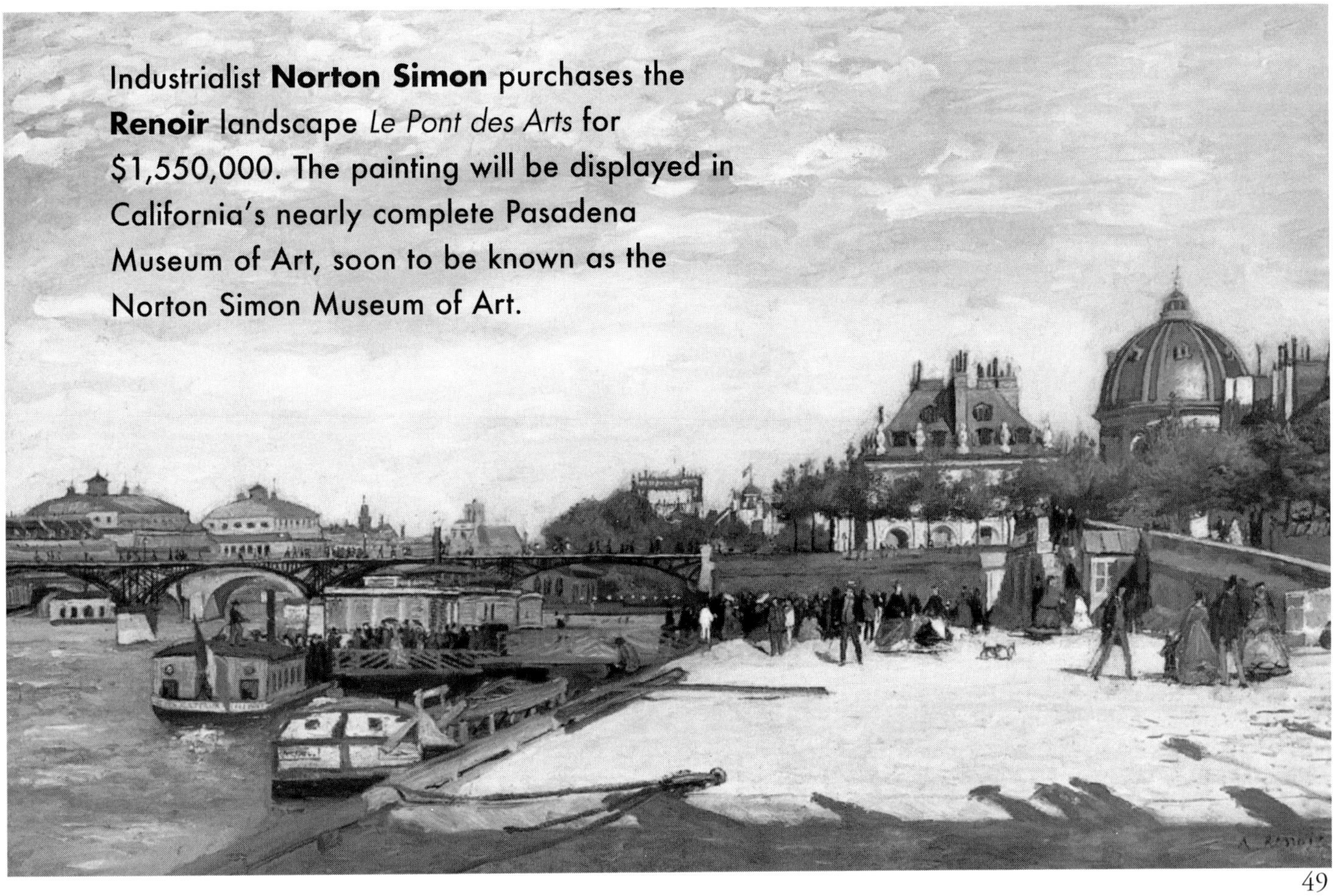

1968 ADVERTISEMENT

ERLE STANLEY

GARDNER

AGATHA

CHRISTIE

and more!

NINE great mysteries for only $1

9 Great Mysteries WORTH $32.95 (in Publishers' Original Editions) Yours for only $1

AS A NEW MEMBER

$11.95 in Publ. Eds.

YOU GET 6 Perry Masons

in these full-size, full-length, hard-bound books

❶ The Case of the WORRIED WAITRESS
Perry Mason's pretty client is charged with *murderous assault*. And the only one who can save her is *BLIND!*

❷ The Case of the BEAUTIFUL BEGGAR
Who *murdered* Daphne? Perry Mason can't figure it out. Then . . . Daphne seems to make a *drastic recovery!*

❸ The Case of the TROUBLED TRUSTEE
Dutton was with Palmer *the very hour* Palmer died. Dutton's gun *killed him!* Can Perry ever save him NOW?

❹ The Case of the HORRIFIED HEIRS
Perry Mason's client met Mrs. Trent only once. But a mutual "friend" WANTS TO *MURDER* THEM *BOTH!*

❺ The Case of the PHANTOM FORTUNE
Perry Mason is forced to *defend himself* when a raging D.A. accuses him of *framing an attempted MURDER!*

❻ The Case of the DARING DIVORCEE
A suspected murder weapon *disappears* and D.A. Hamilton Burger threatens to *put Perry in San Quentin!*

PLUS

Agatha Christie's latest thriller and 2 more top-flight mysteries in this big "3-in-1" Volume

❼ AT BERTRAM'S HOTEL
by Agatha Christie
Jane Marple tracks down the leader of a brazen, million-dollar train robbery — *an elderly, absent-minded Vicar?!*

❽ A BUSINESS OF BODIES
by Stanton Forbes
A funeral director is MURDERED by a lethal formaldehyde cocktail! And the KILLER may be your *very BEST FRIEND!*

❾ CONCEAL AND DISGUISE
by Henry Kane
Can a top society doctor become an ASSASSIN — and take part in a *DEADLY INTERNATIONAL DOUBLE-CROSS?*

Nine great mysteries—worth $32.95—Yours for only $1.00

THRILL to tense courtroom battles, spellbinding action, baffling clues! You get *six* of Erle Stanley Gardner's best Perry Mason mysteries — in six full-size, full-length, hard-bound books. You also get Agatha Christie's latest thriller — PLUS — 2 MORE new full-length mysteries in a big Triple-Volume. These nine mysteries would cost $32.95 in the publishers' original editions — but YOU get ALL NINE of them for only $1.00 as your introduction to the many advantages of membership in The Detective Book Club.

The Best NEW Mysteries — for LESS than 97¢ each!

Out of the 300 or more new detective books that come out every year, the Club selects the very "cream of the crop" — by outstanding authors like Erle Stanley Gardner, Agatha Christie, A. A. Fair, Mignon G. Eberhart, John Creasey and Van Wyck Mason. All THESE and many other famous authors have had their books selected by the Club. Many are members themselves.

Club selections are ALL newly published books. As a member, you get THREE of them complete in one handsomely bound Triple Volume (a $10.50 to $11.95 value in publishers' original editions) for ONLY $2.89.

Take ONLY The Books You Want

You do NOT have to take a volume every month. You receive a free copy of the Club's "Preview" which will fully describe all coming selections and you may reject any volume before or after receiving it. NO money in advance; NO membership fees. You may cancel your membership at any time.

You Enjoy These Five Advantages

(1) You get the cream of the finest BRAND-NEW detective books — by the best authors. (2) You save between $7 and $9 off the cost of publishers' regular retail editions. (3) You take ONLY the books you want. (4) The volumes are fresh and clean — delivered to your door. (5) They are so well-printed and bound that they grow into a library you'll be proud to own.

SEND NO MONEY

Mail Coupon for ALL NINE Mysteries

Simply mail coupon promptly and we will send you at once the SIX Perry Mason bafflers—PLUS the THREE OTHER exciting mysteries described on this page. But don't delay. Mail coupon NOW to:

DETECTIVE BOOK CLUB

THE DETECTIVE BOOK CLUB
Roslyn, L. I., New York 11576

SEND NO MONEY — JUST MAIL COUPON 7-297

THE DETECTIVE BOOK CLUB **7-AZ**
Roslyn, L. I., New York 11576

Please enroll me as a member and send me at once the SIX full-length, hard-bound editions of Perry Mason thrillers, PLUS the brand-new 3-in-1 volume Club selection containing Agatha Christie's latest and 2 more great mysteries. I enclose NO MONEY IN ADVANCE; within a week after receiving my books, I will either return them all and owe nothing, or keep ALL SEVEN volumes, containing NINE first-rate mystery stories, for the special new-member introductory price of ONLY $1.00 (plus a few cents mailing charges).

As a member, I am to receive advance descriptions of all future selections, but am not obligated to buy any. For each future triple-volume I decide to keep, I will send you only $2.89 (plus a few cents mailing charges). I may reject any volume before or after I receive it, and I may cancel my membership at any time. (Books shipped in U.S.A. only).

Mr. / Mrs. / Miss ....
(PLEASE PRINT PLAINLY)

Address ....

City & State .... ZIP CODE ZONE NO.

Books

Arthur C. Clarke

Technological, political, and cultural revolution come together in the experimental styles and themes of some of this year's biggest books. NASA's frontier-expanding exploration of space is refracted through the eyes of **Arthur C. Clarke** in his *2001: A Space Odyssey.* Clarke's novel, which complements the film, transcends the sci-fi genre to pose fundamental questions about our origins, existence, and future.

Star Quest, the first novel by **Dean R. Koontz**, is published. Koontz embarks on a long career, with loyal readers enjoying his books in 38 languages.

Erich von Daniken credits extraterrestrials with the origin of earthly religions in his *Chariots of the Gods,* connecting ancient texts and artifacts with spacecraft from other worlds.

Tom Wolfe's *The Electric Kool-Aid Acid Test* explores another frontier, inner space, in his psychedelic "new journalism" romp through the misadventures of author **Ken Kesey** (*One Flew Over the Cuckoo's Nest*) and his cohorts, known as the Merry Pranksters. Wolfe's book chronicles the band's cross-country journey through middle America while high on LSD. Another Wolfe novel, *The Pump House Gang,* is published concurrently with *Acid Test.*

Hallucinogenic peyote cacti introduce "back to nature" counterculturists to Native American spiritual life in **N. Scott Momaday**'s *House Made of Dawn,* which will earn him the Pulitzer Prize in 1969.

Moralizing British author **Malcolm Muggeridge** complains that "the novel has sunk without a trace into a slough of sex and slush." Perhaps he has read **John Updike**'s *Couples*—a tale of marriage in a Massachusetts village, which is called "the best-written dirty book since *The Decameron*"—or **Gore Vidal**'s *Myra Breckinridge,* a satirical novel about a transsexual starlet in Hollywood.

Muggeridge's lament may be borne out in the *New York Times Book Review,* whose annual Christmas list of 10 books "of particular significance and excellence" includes only one work of fiction this year—*The First Circle,* by **Alexander Solzhenitsyn**.

Alexander Solzhenitsyn

Richard Brautigan

Norman Mailer

Books

Airport
Arthur Hailey

The Armies of the Night
Norman Mailer

Asimov's Mysteries
Isaac Asimov

Black Easter
James Blish

A Book of Mermaids
Ruth Manning-Sanders

Cancer Ward
Alexander Solzhenitsyn

Cocksure
Mordecai Richler

Colonel Sun
Robert Markham

Conan the Avenger
Robert E. Howard, et al

Couples
John Updike

Do Androids Dream of Electric Sheep?
Philip K. Dick

Enderby Outside
Anthony Burgess

The God Machine
Martin Caidin

I Am Mary Dunne
Brian Moore

The Ice-Cream Headache
James Jones

In Watermelon Sugar
Richard Brautigan

Indian Country
Dorothy M. Johnson

The Military Philosophers
Anthony Powell

Myra Breckinridge
Gore Vidal

Nightmares and Daydreams
Nelson Bond

Not Before Time
John Brunner

Preserve and Protect
Allen Drury

The Salzburg Connection
Helen MacInnes

A Small Town in Germany
John Le Carré

Testimony of Two Men
Taylor Caldwell

Tigers Are Better-Looking
Jean Rhys

Illustrator Robert Crumb, better known simply as **R. Crumb**, *launches a comics revolution with the first issues of his self-published "underground" magazine,* Zap Comix. *Anti-establishment and lampooning just about everything, they introduce his galaxy of characters including Mr. Natural, Whiteman, Devil Girl, and Fritz the Cat.*

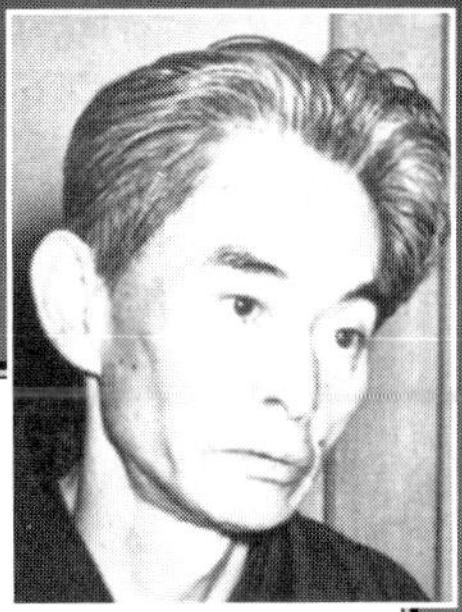

Kawabata

Nobel Prize for Literature

YASUNARI KAWABATA, Japan

Pulitzer Prizes

FICTION

The Confessions of Nat Turner WILLIAM STYRON

NONFICTION

Rousseau and Revolution WILL AND ARIEL DURANT

POETRY

The Hard Hours ANTHONY HECHT

Newbery Medal (Children's)

From the Mixed-Up Files of Mrs. Basil E. Frankweiler
E. L. KONIGSBURG

Prix Goncourt

Les Fruits de l'hiver BERNARD CLAVEL

Viareggio Prize

La Controfigura LIBERO BIGIARETTI

Hugo Award (Science Fiction)

Lord of Light ROGER ZELAZNY

American Academy of Arts & Letters Poetry Gold Medal

W. H. AUDEN

Farewell and Good Night:

American author **Upton Sinclair** dies at age 90. Sinclair, who wrote more than 90 books over the course of his career, made his biggest literary splash with *The Jungle*, a book revealing squalid conditions in the U.S. meat-packing industry.

John Steinbeck, one of the most well-known American writers, dies at age 66 of a heart attack. Steinbeck, winner of the Nobel Prize in Literature and the Pulitzer Prize for *The Grapes of Wrath*, reportedly wrote a note to his doctor saying he felt deeply "in his bones that he would not survive his physical death, and that the biological end of his life was the final end to it."

Steinbeck

Architecture

Ford Foundation Building

The **Architecture Firm Award** is the highest honor that the American Institute of Architects can bestow on a firm for consistently producing distinguished architecture. **I.M. Pei & Partners** take the award this year. According to the AIA, "the firm's work has consistently reflected sensitivity, technical skill and an awareness of the human and material factors that must be combined to produce outstanding architecture."

The **Standard Bank Centre** skyscraper in Johannesburg, South Africa, is actually built from the top down. After the core is complete, floors are suspended with the top floors being added first.

Marcel Lajos Bruer wins the **AIA** (American Institute of Architects) **Gold Medal.**

The **Royal Gold Medal**, awarded annually by the Royal Institute of British Architects in recognition of an individual's or group's substantial contribution to international architecture, is won by **Richard Buckminster Fuller**.

The **Architecture Critics Award**, presented for the first time this year, goes to **Lewis Mumford**, author of several histories of architecture. The **Medal of Honor** goes to **Kevin Roche**, designer of the new Ford Foundation Building in New York City.

The **Neue Nationalgalerie** at the Kulturforum, a museum for classical modern art in Berlin, is designed by **Ludwig Mies van der Rohe** and opens this year. The view of the ground floor shows the play of light off the reflective floor and the red LCD tracks on the ceiling. Although almost all of the display area is underground, the lobby is still the most dramatic with walls made almost entirely of glass. Rohe is considered the master of the modern movement in architecture.

Lake Point Tower, a high-rise residential building on Lake Michigan in downtown Chicago, is also the only skyscraper east of Lake Shore Drive. At 600 feet, it is the highest apartment building in the world.

Radio telecommunication tower, Heinrich-Hertz-Turm, is Hamburg, Germany's tallest building

Making cities liveable as well as beautiful becomes a major architectural goal throughout the year. British economist **Barbara Ward** says, "When we talk of the cities, we talk of the future of humanity." Ward warns that continued unplanned and chaotic growth of cities might bring violence, revolt, and collapse to civilization The systematic approach to urban planning, she says is "the only adequate intellectual response to the challenge of the urban revolution."

1969 Dodge Polara.
Totally new, it is. Expensive, it isn't.

If you're looking for a big, luxurious new car that sports a low price, look no farther. 1969 Dodge Polara. With such standard items as foam-padded seats, carpeting, and a 230-hp V8. Not to mention an all-new instrument panel and concealed windshield wipers. Why wait, big car lovers? This is your year. 1969 Dodge Polara.

In The News

Still recovering from the 1963 assassination of President **John F. Kennedy** and 1965's slaying of civil rights firebrand **Malcolm X**, the nation and the world are further staggered by the loss of Reverend **Martin Luther King, Jr.** in April and Senator **Robert F. "Bobby" Kennedy** in June, both felled by assassins' bullets near the end of a decade in which hope increasingly seems to give way to violence.

The Vietnam War: A Growing Dread

The Vietnam War—the longest war in U.S. history—continues abroad while Americans are increasingly polarized at home. With the U.S. death count approaching 30,000, protests on the rise, and the war looming as the number one election topic, President **Lyndon B. Johnson**'s administration engages North Vietnam in peace talks. But expectations for successful negotiations are low and LBJ's refusal to escalate the war by sending in more troops is widely seen as an admission that victory is illusory and that the war is a lost cause.

A U.S. soldier walks through a burning Viet Cong base camp in My Tho, Vietnam.

U.S. TROOPS PUSH TANKS THROUGH JUNGLE

North of Saigon, near the Cambodian border, heavy fighting is spearheaded by U.S. tanks pushing up from the south.

A "corduroy road" is laid to help speed progress. Paratroops are also part of this drive, designed to clear out a longtime Viet Cong stronghold. American fighting men suffer heavy casualties during the campaign.

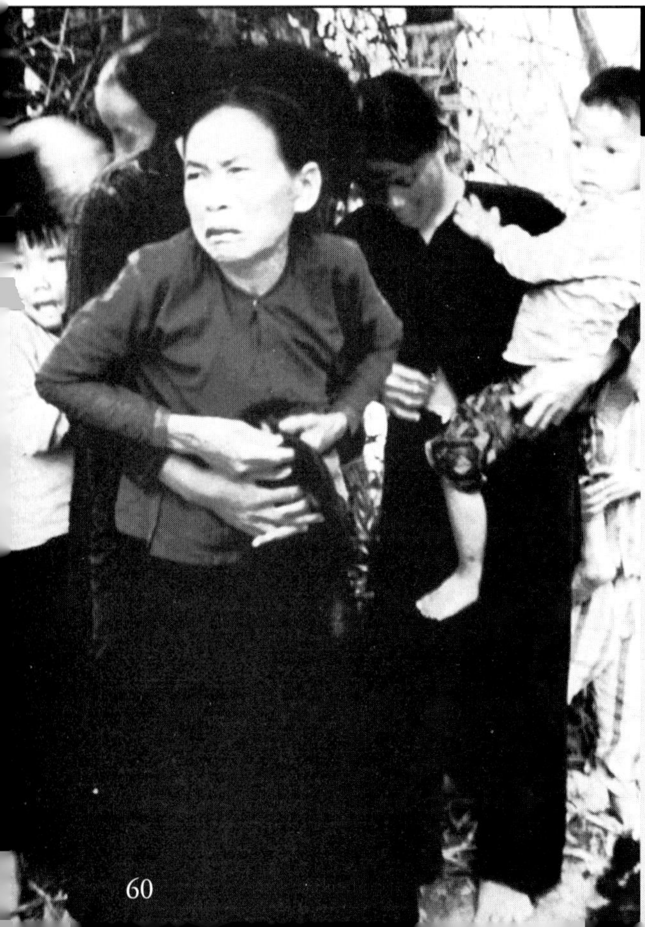

Massacre at My Lai

American public support for the war, already at low ebb, is stretched to the breaking point by the revelation of the massacre of unarmed Vietnamese by American soldiers at the village of My Lai on March 16, 1968. The public only learns of the event over a year after the fact. News of the carnage sparks international outrage.

U.S. infantrymen enter the village in the morning, searching for insurgents. Finding none but suspecting Viet Cong are in the vicinity, soldiers go berserk, laying waste to the community and engaging in acts of brutality and torture. Ultimately 504 people are slaughtered, mainly women and children.

In 1971 Lieutenant **William Calley** is convicted of premeditated murder for ordering the killings.

Women and children cower at My Lai before being killed.

VIETNAM

1968

JANUARY

The Tet Offensive begins as Viet Cong forces launch a series of surprise attacks across South Vietnam. The campaign ends a month later with the recapture of Hue.

Viet Cong soldiers attack the United States Embassy in Saigon.

FEBRUARY A Viet Cong officer is executed by Nguyen Ngoc Loan, a South Vietnamese police chief. A Pulitzer Prize-winning photo of the event makes news around the world, swaying U.S. public opinion against the war.

MARCH The First Battle of Saigon begins.

JULY South Vietnamese opposition leader Truong Dinh Dzu is sentenced to prison for advocating the formation of a coalition government.

OCTOBER Operation Sealord - U.S. and South Vietnamese forces launch a new operation in the Mekong Delta.

The U.S. Department of Defense announces that it will send 24,000 troops back to Vietnam for involuntary second tours.

Citing progress in the Paris peace talks, President Johnson orders a cessation of "all air, naval, and artillery bombardment of North Vietnam" effective November 1.

NOVEMBER Operation Commando Hunt commences to interdict men and supplies on the Ho Chi Minh Trail. 3 million tons of bombs are dropped on Laos, slowing but not seriously disrupting trail operations.

Men enjoy a moment of relaxation after a hard day.

A trooper from the 1st Cavalry Division keeps track of the remaining duration of his tour of duty on his "short time" helmet.

THE WAR AT HOME

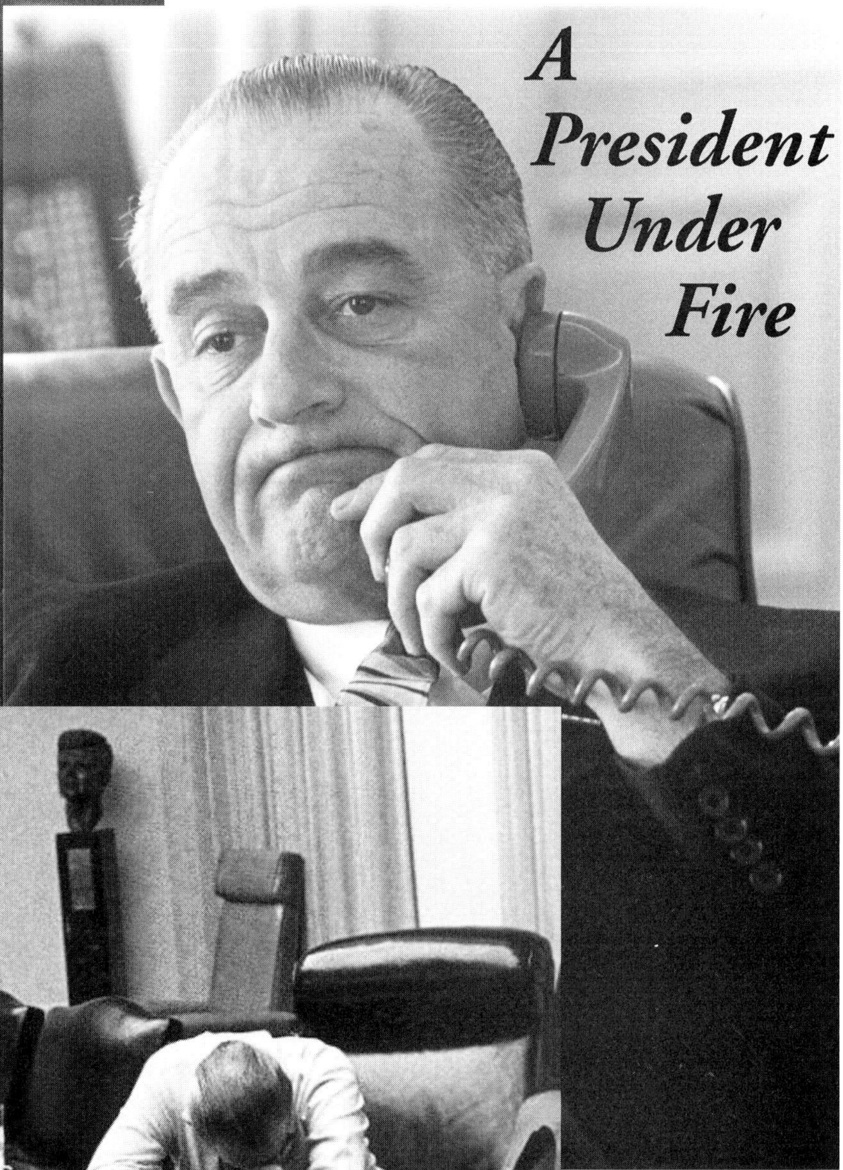

A President Under Fire

The first few years of President **Lyndon Baines Johnson**'s presidency see great strides toward the achievement of his vision of a "Great Society." In 1964, seeking to eliminate racial segregation, he overcomes southern resistance to push through the Civil Rights Act and, the following year, the Voting Rights Act. He could count the establishment of Medicare and Medicaid, as well as gains in education, urban renewal, and the war on poverty as successes. But the Vietnam War grinds on with no end in sight, increasingly consuming him. His popularity plummets. Satisfying neither the "hawks" nor the "doves," he opts for a middle path of containment while pursuing a peace settlement.

Unable to leave the White House without facing protesters chanting "Hey, hey, LBJ, how many kids did you kill today," and losing control of a fractured Democratic party, an exhausted president addresses the nation on March 31st. Television viewers are stunned when he unexpectedly announces ***"I shall not seek, and I will not accept the nomination of my party for another term as your President."***

Politics and World Events

ANTIWAR PROTESTS

The Columbia protest

Student protesters at Columbia University in New York City occupy administration buildings and shut down the university, taking three school officials hostage for 24 hours. After six days, 1,000 police clear the buildings in a violent clash with the students.

A group of Catholics—including Revs. **Daniel** and **Philip Berrigan** and various priests and nuns—enter the Selective Service offices in Catonsville, Maryland, burning draft records with napalm as a protest against the Vietnam War. The "Catonsville Nine" are tried in federal court and found guilty of destruction of U.S. property.

A demonstration in London's Grosvenor Square against U.S. involvement in the Vietnam War leads to violence. 91 police are injured and 200 protesters arrested.

Veterans for Peace March on the Pentagon.

A Turbulent Election

March 12 President **Lyndon B. Johnson** barely edges out antiwar candidate U.S. Senator **Eugene J. McCarthy** in the New Hampshire Democratic primary.

March 16 U.S. Senator **Robert F. Kennedy** enters the race for the Democratic Party presidential nomination.

March 31 Johnson announces he will not seek reelection.

June 5 Kennedy is assassinated in Los Angeles by **Sirhan Sirhan** after winning the California primary.

August 5-8 The Republican National Convention in Miami nominates **Richard M. Nixon** for President and **Spiro T. Agnew** for Vice President.

August 26-29 A deeply divided and chaotic Democratic National Convention in Chicago nominates Vice President **Hubert H. Humphrey** for President and U.S. Senator **Edmund Muskie** for Vice President.

The convention is disrupted by violent police actions waged against demonstrators outside the event. Eight of the arrested protesters — **Abbie Hoffman**, **Tom Hayden**, **Dave Dellinger**, **Rennie Davis**, **John Froines**, **Jerry Rubin**, **Lee Weiner**, and Black Panther **Bobby Seale** — are charged with conspiracy to incite a riot. The "Chicago 7" (Seale ends up being tried separately) are acquitted in 1970.

November 5 Republican challenger Nixon defeats Humphrey and American Independent Party candidate **George C. Wallace** to win the U.S. presidential election.

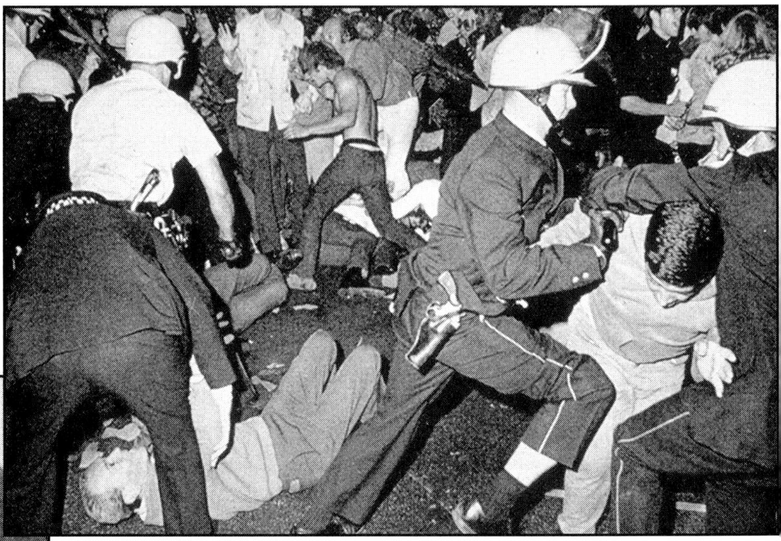

Above: Protesters clash with police at Chicago Democratic Convention.

Above: Richard M. Nixon campaigns.

Right: Lyndon Johnson meets with candidate Nixon at the White House, July 26, 1968.

CIVIL RIGHTS

The cycle of black poverty, despair and urban turmoil—marked in the mid-'60s by the Harlem and Watts riots—reaches a crescendo in 1967, with violent outbursts spreading across the country. "White flight" accelerates as urban white residents increasingly flee to the suburbs, leaving America's inner cities even more isolated. News of the assassination of Rev. **Martin Luther King, Jr.** sparks new unrest. Riots erupt in Chicago, Cleveland, Baltimore, and Washington, D.C. King's doctrine of nonviolent confrontation continues to be challenged by those advocating black militancy and the concept of armed self-defense, as exemplified by the Black Panthers.

At the same time, some activists see force offering diminishing returns and argue for a new strategy. In the face of declining membership, the Black Panther Party for Self-Defense officially shortens its name to the Black Panther Party and ramps up its focus on social programs. Seeking to downplay its violent image, members are forbidden to bear arms in public.

Damage to a store following the riots in Washington, D.C., April 16, 1968.

CIVIL RIGHTS

A civil rights protest at a whites-only bowling alley in Orangeburg, South Carolina is broken up with force by highway patrolmen, leading to the deaths of three college students on February 8th.

The Medal of Honor is posthumously bestowed on **James Anderson, Jr.***, the first African American U.S. Marine to receive the award.*

A shootout between eight Black Panther Party members, including **Eldridge Cleaver**, and Oakland police on April 6th results in several arrests and the death of 17-year-old Panther **Bobby Hutton**.

President **Lyndon B. Johnson** signs the Civil Rights Act of 1968 on April 11th.

Black militants led by **Fred Evans** engage in a fierce July gunfight with police in Cleveland, Ohio. Seven die in the event known as the "Glenville Shootout" and several days of rioting ensue.

Tommie Smith *and* ***John Carlos****, gold and bronze medalists respectively in the 200-meter run at the Mexico City Summer Olympic Games, raise their arms in a gloved black power salute on the winner's podium on October 16th. Smith and Carlos are suspended from the U.S. team for their action.*

THE PUEBLO INCIDENT

On January 23rd, 1968 the USS *Pueblo*, a U.S. Navy technical research ship dispatched to monitor Soviet naval activity, is attacked and boarded by crews of the Democratic People's Republic of Korea (North Korea). One U.S. sailor is killed and the Americans are bound, blindfolded and beaten. Crew members are taken into custody and subsequently tortured, with *Pueblo* Commander **Lloyd M. Bucher** being subjected to a mock firing squad in an effort to make him confess to spying.

The Korean claim that *Pueblo* violated her territorial waters is disputed by the ship's crew and the U.S. government. Nevertheless, the U.S. provides the Koreans with a written admission that *Pueblo* had indeed been spying, and an assurance that the U.S. would discontinue spying activity. The 82 remaining crew members are released exactly 11 months after their capture. The USS *Pueblo* remains docked in North Korea where it is a popular tourist attraction.

The crew of the Pueblo *upon their repatriation by North Korea, December 23, 1968.*

The Central Intelligence Agency's Phoenix Program—designed to identify and capture, assassinate and infiltrate the civilian infrastructure supporting Vietnam's Marxist insurgency—is officially established.

The Congress of the United States repeals the requirement for a gold reserve to back U.S. currency.

MILITARY and NUCLEAR WOES

January 21: A U.S. B-52 Stratofortress crashes in Greenland with weapons-grade plutonium aboard. U.S. specialists hurry to remove all traces of military technology. Hundreds of local civilians are engaged to remove contaminated snow and ice.

January 25: The Israeli submarine INS *Dakar*, just purchased from the British Royal Navy, sinks in the eastern Mediterranean Sea. 69 crew are killed.

January 27: The French submarine *Minerve* sinks in the Mediterranean Sea with 52 men aboard.

March 14: Nerve gas leaks from the U.S. Army Dugway Proving Ground near Skull Valley, Utah.

May 22: The U.S. nuclear-powered submarine *Scorpion* sinks in over 10,000 feet of water with 99 men aboard, 400 miles southwest of the Azores.

Prague Spring

Beginning in January, Czech Communist Party leader **Alexander Dubcek** embarks on a course of political liberalization unheard of in any Warsaw Pact country, to include increased freedom of the press, greater availability of consumer goods, and the promise of a democratic multi-party government.

Concerned with the rising tide of anti-communist sentiment beginning to emerge in its satellite state, Soviet leadership attempts to limit the spread of freedom in Czechoslovakia through negotiation. When that fails, armies from five Eastern Bloc armies and thousands of Soviet tanks invade city streets in August, resulting in the deaths of 72 Czechs and sparking a wave of emigration, which is quickly quelled. Despite brave resistance from many Czechs, communist authority is reasserted.

Soviet tanks enter Prague.

The Politics of Revolution

While Eastern Europe strains under the yoke of communism, activists in Western Europe attempt to move their governments to the left, sometimes through violent means.

Baader

Meinhof

Ensslin

In April, bombs placed by "communist urban guerillas" **Andreas Baader** and his girlfriend **Gudrun Ensslin** explode at midnight in two department stores in Frankfurt, Germany. The pair are later arrested and sentenced to three years for arson.

In the same month, German left-wing students blockade the publishing offices of Springer Press in Berlin. Many are arrested, including **Ulrike Meinhof**, who would later team with Andreas Baader to form the Red Army Faction—otherwise known as the notorious Baader-Meinhof Gang. Leftist student leader **Rudi Dutschke** is the subject of an assassination attempt. Dutschke survives, but dies of his brain injuries 11 years later.

Meanwhile, France is undergoing political upheaval of its own. In March, **Daniel Cohn-Bendit** and seven other students occupy administrative offices at the University of Nanterre. "May of '68" becomes a battle cry of resistance for many Parisians. Political actions cause some to believe that a leftist revolution is starting as student and worker strikes come close to bringing down the French government.

EUROPE

George Brown, Britain's Foreign Secretary, resigns in March over rumors about his drinking and unavailability during a political crisis.

Powell

Controversial English politician **Enoch Powell** delivers his "Rivers of Blood" speech in April, in which he warns against unchecked immigration and denounces anti-discrimination legislation.

Austin Currie, Member of Parliament at Stormont in Northern Ireland, joins in a June protest that includes house squatting as a protest against discrimination in housing allocations.

An October civil rights march in Derry, Northern Ireland, attended by several Stormont and British MPs, is violently suppressed by the Royal Ulster Constabulary.

Engineer **Giorgio Rosa** declares the independence of his Republic of Rose Island, a man-made platform in the Adriatic Sea off Rimini, Italy. The Italian navy demolishes it with explosives.

Rosa's island

Marcelo Caetano becomes Prime Minister of Portugal.

A September referendum in Greece gives more power to the military junta known as the "Regime of the Colonels."

France explodes its first hydrogen bomb, becoming the world's fifth nuclear power.

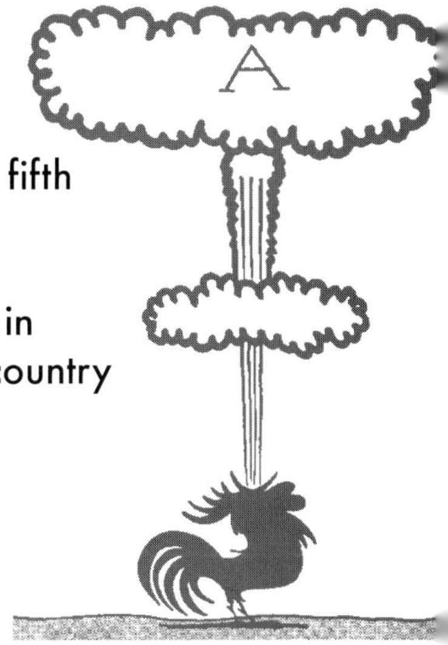

Administrative reform in Romania divides the country into 39 counties.

The gift that's meant to be cracked

The more your child cracks open and uses The New Book of Knowledge, the more valuable this gift becomes. Not so with the usual toys. They're fun while they last. But the minute they're cracked, they're forgotten. The New Book of Knowledge is hardly the usual gift. It invites your child to use it. Every page, article and illustration in this all new, educator-approved encyclopedia is designed to capture your child's imagination, to lead him to explore and absorb the knowledge that will last forever.

The encyclopedia that knows what's going on at school

Before we wrote a word of The New Book of Knowledge, we studied the changing methods and matter of elementary school curricula. We developed a formula to test the readability of our articles and tested our theories in classrooms across the country. The result? The New Book of Knowledge provides the direct continuation into your home of the way your child is taught and what he is taught in school. It is the much-needed link between home and school.

Free color preview of The New Book of Knowledge

To give you an idea of what makes this new 20-volume encyclopedia unique, we've prepared a 28-page color booklet. In it you'll find a sampling of the 22,400 illustrations in The New Book of Knowledge (13,700 in color—more than in any other encyclopedia). You'll see how the words, maps and pictures work together to involve your child in learning and make him want to know what he must know today.

Our booklet's called "The Magic Carpet" and we'll send it to you free as soon as you send us this coupon.

The New Book of Knowledge.

A publication of Grolier Incorporated. Cash price $200 plus handling and shipping. Budget terms available.

The New Book of Knowledge,
Putnam Valley, N.Y. 10579

Send for the Magic Carpet, your free 28 page color preview of The New Book of Knowledge. See what six years of research and over seven million dollars can do to help your child know more. Send the coupon today, so your child can have a brighter tomorrow.

Name__________

Address__________ City__________

State__________ County__________ Zip__________

There are__________ children in my family, ages__________

LO 11-12-68

Saddam Hussein plays a key role in a July coup which brings the Baath Party to power in **Iraq**. Hussein becomes Vice Chairman of the Revolutionary Council.

A series of border clashes occur between **Israel** and **Jordan**.

Kingston, **Jamaica** is shaken by the so-called "Rodney Riots," provoked by the government's banning of activist, scholar and advocate for the poor **Walter Rodney** from the country.

Pierre Elliott Trudeau becomes **Canada**'s 15th Prime Minister.

Mao Zedong advocates educated youth in urban **China** to be reeducated in the country, marking the start of the "Up to the mountains and down to the villages" movement.

Island nation **Mauritius** achieves independence from **Britain** on March 12th.

South Pacific island nation **Nauru** declares independence from **Australia** on January 31st.

Try the <u>complete</u> surprise . . . Carroll Shelby's COBRA GT

Carroll Shelby reasons that a *true* GT needs *everything* for high performance pleasure, comfort and safety engineered right in, not just offered as afterthought options. That's why his Cobra GT is a *complete* surprise to those who see it and drive it for the first time. ☐ Surprise number one is style. Subtle changes in grille, hood, sides, rear deck add a fresh, exclusive look. Interior luxury follows through with deep-bucket seats, walnut-grain appliques, front seat center console-armrest, courtesy lights, full instrumentation. ☐ Naturally, you expect performance . . . but the GT 500's Shelby-ized 428 cubic inch V-8 rewrites the performance charts with surprising smoothness. A 302 V-8 is Shelby-prepared for the GT 350. Special wide-path tires, 16-to-1 power steering, modified suspension and adjustable super-duty shocks deliver firm control but with enough velvet to make an all-day trip a pleasure. ☐ Safety features are engineered-in, too. These include an overhead safety bar and inertia-reel shoulder harnesses, impact-absorbing steering wheel, dual braking system. ☐ By engineering his other surprises into the great-to-start-with Mustang, Carroll Shelby's biggest surprise is the small price. ☐ Your Shelby dealer will prove just how big *that* surprise can be.

Shelby COBRA GT 350/500 POWER BY Ford

AFRICA

Congo President **Joseph Mobutu** has Congolese revolutionary and former education minister **Pierre Mulele** brutally tortured, limbs amputated, and finally executed, all in public.

Mobutu

Mulele

The small, landlocked south African nation **Swaziland** becomes independent of Britain on September 6th.

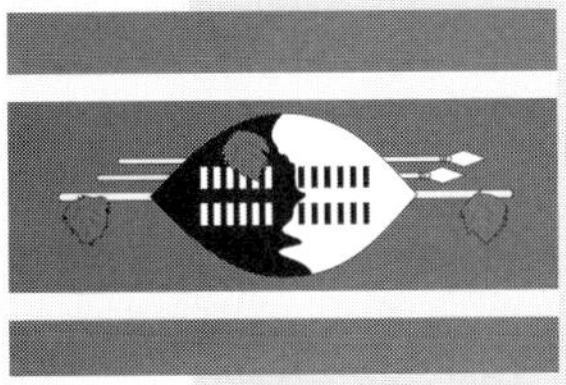

Equatorial Guinea receives its independence from Spain on October 12th.

LATIN AMERICA

A student demonstration ends in a bloodbath on October 2nd at La Plaza de las Tres Culturas in Mexico City, **Mexico,** 10 days before the inauguration of the 1968 Summer Olympics. 200-300 are killed in the so-called "Tlatelolco massacre."

A military coup d'etat on October 11th in **Panama,** led by Col. **Boris Martinez** and Col. **Omar Torrijos**, overthrows the democratically elected but autocratic government of President **Arnulfo Arias**.

Omar Torrijos with Panamanian farmers.

Luis A. Ferré is elected Governor of **Puerto Rico**.

Brazilian president **Artur da Costa e Silva** decrees the Fifth Institutional Act, which lasts until 1978 and effectively establishes a military dictatorship.

Any carpet can cover the floor. Ozite decorates it!

New kitchen carpet in multicolor patterns. As durable as famous Ozite Outdoor-Indoor Carpet. No waxing, polishing. Rubber back. Attractive *Grille Petite* and *Confetti* patterns.

Soft, warm, quiet Carpet Tiles. 12" squares. Rubber back. Many colors. Special method lets you install most tiles *loose*, without adhesive. For spills, pick up, wash off, put back!

Outdoor-Indoor Carpet in colorful patterns. Choose from *Brick, Mosaic* and *Wrought Iron* patterns in variety of colors. If this carpet holds up outdoors, think how it wears indoors!

All made with stain-resistant Vectra fiber. Ozite has the most complete, proven line of carpet products for outdoors and indoors. Insist on Ozite! Look for the name on the back.

Use your imagination with...

Ozite® CARPET PRODUCTS made with Vectra® OLEFIN FIBER

Ozite® is the registered trademark of the Ozite Corporation, Merchandise Mart, Chicago, Illinois. Vectra® olefin fiber is manufactured by Enjay Fibers and Laminates Company, Odenton, Maryland, a division of Enjay Chemical Company. Enjay makes fiber, not carpets

People

This year sees its share of death, none felt more keenly by the American public than the assassinations of Dr. Martin Luther King, Jr. and Robert F. Kennedy.

Dr. Martin Luther King, Jr. became the youngest man to be awarded the Nobel Peace Prize in 1964 for his devotion to promoting nonviolence, equal treatment for all, and world peace. As one of the greatest leaders of the American civil rights movement, Dr. King educated and inspired countless generations of Americans. Tragedy strikes on April 4, 1968, and the world loses one of its greatest orators when Dr. King is assassinated by James Earl Ray on the balcony outside of his room at the Lorraine Motel in Memphis, Tennessee.

Dr. King's family lead his funeral procession on April 9.

Dr. King is posthumously awarded the Presidential Medal of Freedom by Jimmy Carter in 1977. In 1986 his birthday, January 15, is declared a United States holiday – only the fourth federal holiday to honor an individual. Dr. King was known as something of a fatalist and remarked after shots were fired while he preached in a small Georgia church in 1962: *"It may get me crucified. I may even die. But I want it said even if I die in the struggle, that he died to make me free."*

James Earl Ray, convicted of the assassination, also has the notoriety of having been twice placed on the FBI's Ten Most Wanted Fugitives list.

"We've had difficult times in the past. We will have difficult times in the future. It is not the end of violence; it is not the end of lawlessness; it is not the end of disorder."

Robert F. Kennedy's words as he broke the news of Dr. King's assassination to a group of African Americans in Indianapolis. The large gathering was a planned political rally in his run for the Democratic nomination for President in 1968.

Frankie Lymon, lead singer of the Teenagers, dies at age 25. Although Frankie Lymon & the Teenagers are together only 18 months, they are renowned for being one of rock music's earliest successes and for being rock's first all-teenage act. Their first single, "Why Do Fools Fall in Love," is their biggest hit. The group falls apart in 1957 when Lymon goes solo. After years of declining popularity, Lymon signs with the Big Apple label in 1968. "Celebrating" his return to the spotlight, Lymon takes heroin and is found dead of an overdose. "I'm Sorry" and "Seabreeze," recorded for Big Apple before Lymon's death, are released later this year.

Soviet cosmonaut Yuri Alekseyevich Gagarin dies at age 34. Gagarin staked his claim to fame in 1961 when he became the first human in space and the first to orbit the Earth. On March 27, he and his instructor are killed on a routine training flight near Kirzhach, Russia. Although uncertainly surrounds the cause of the crash, a later inquest puts the blame on turbulence and poor weather conditions.

Blank Panther Party member Bobby Hutton, or "Lil' Bobby," is killed by Oakland police after a gunfight. Wounded in the same incident is a Black Panther Party leader, Eldridge Cleaver. The Panthers claim Hutton was trying to surrender, but police say he was trying to escape. Both sides agree Hutton was unarmed.

Cleaver's book *Soul on Ice* is published this year. The book is his view of the effects of racism which he wrote while in prison. Cleaver had been released from prison in 1966 and is on parole when the shootout occurs. With his parole revoked he is arrested and charged with assault and attempted murder. Instead of returning to jail in November as scheduled, Cleaver skips out on his $50,000 bail and flees to Mexico.

In June, American artist **Andy Warhol** is shot and seriously wounded. Warhol is declared clinically dead at the hospital, and barely survives doctors' efforts to massage his heart. Valerie Solanas, a 28-year-old actress who works for Warhol, admits she shot him because he refused to film a script she wrote. Solanas suffers from acute paranoia and had previously founded a group (of which she was the only member) called SCUM, or the "Society for Cutting Up Men." Her explanation for the attack: "He had too much control over my life."

Just moments after claiming victory over Eugene McCarthy in the California presidential primary, on June 5, 1968 in the Ambassador Hotel in Los Angeles **Robert F. Kennedy** is assassinated. After addressing his supporters, Kennedy proceeds to walk through the kitchen, shaking hands with hotel staff. Suddenly, 24-year-old Sirhan Sirhan steps in front of him and reportedly yells, "Kennedy, you son of a bitch!" then shoots him with a .22-caliber revolver. A bystander in the back of the room is reported as crying out, "Oh God, it can't happen to this family again!" Kennedy, shot twice in the back and once behind his right ear, is pronounced dead the next day.

Kennedy is returned to New York City, where his body lies in state at St. Patrick's Cathedral in New York for several days before his funeral. His brother Senator Edward M. Kennedy eloquently eulogizes him, saying, "My brother need not be idealized, or enlarged in death beyond what he was in life, to be remembered simply as a good and decent man, who saw wrong and tried to right it, saw suffering and tried to heal it, saw war and tried to stop it. Those of us who loved him and who take him to his rest today, pray that what he was to us and what he wished for others will some day come to pass for all the world. As he said many times, in many parts of this nation, to those he touched and who sought to touch him: 'Some men see things as they are and say why. I dream things that never were and say why not.' "

RFK speaks at the Ambassador Hotel in Los Angeles moments before he is shot.

Kennedy is buried near his brother John in Arlington National Cemetery. His is the only burial to ever take place there at night.

After the assassination, the mandate of the Secret Service is altered to include protection of presidential candidates.

When Kennedy declared his candidacy on March 16, he stated, "I do not run for the presidency merely to oppose any man but to propose new policies. I run because I am convinced that this country is on a perilous course and because I have such strong feelings about what must be done, and I feel that I'm obliged to do all I can."

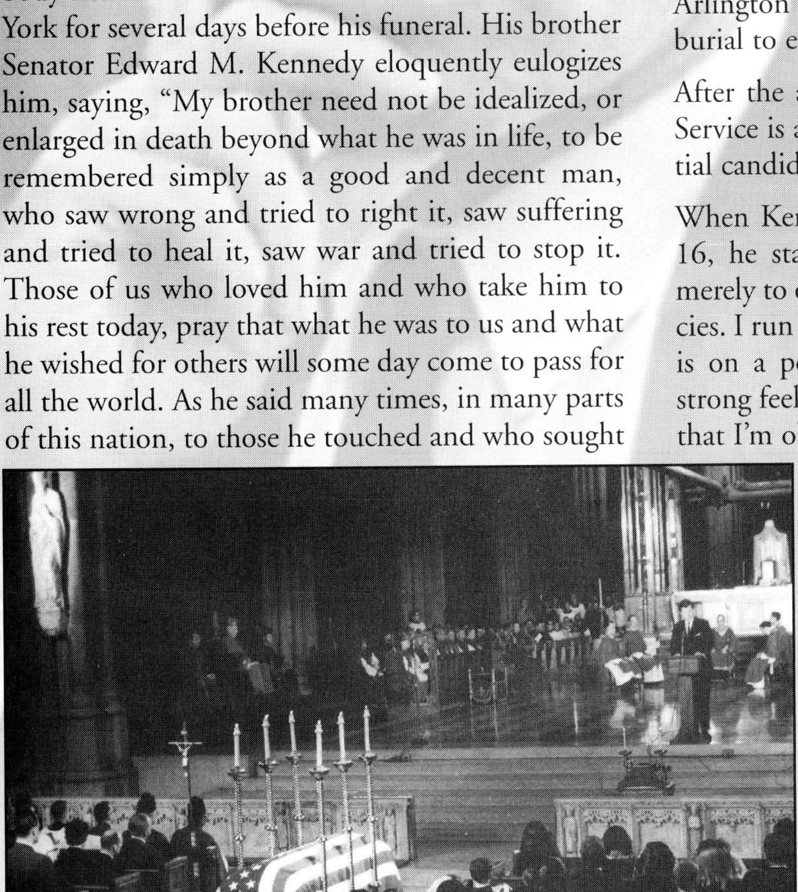
RFK is eulogized by his brother, Senator Edward Kennedy, at St. Patrick's Cathedral.

His ticket was based on racial and economic justice, nonaggression in foreign policy, decentralization of power, and social improvement. He was not popular with the bigwigs of business, who asked him who was going to pay for all his proposed social improvement programs. Kennedy's reply: "You are."

"Some men see things as they are and say why. I dream things that never were and say why not."

THE FAR SIDE OF THE MOON

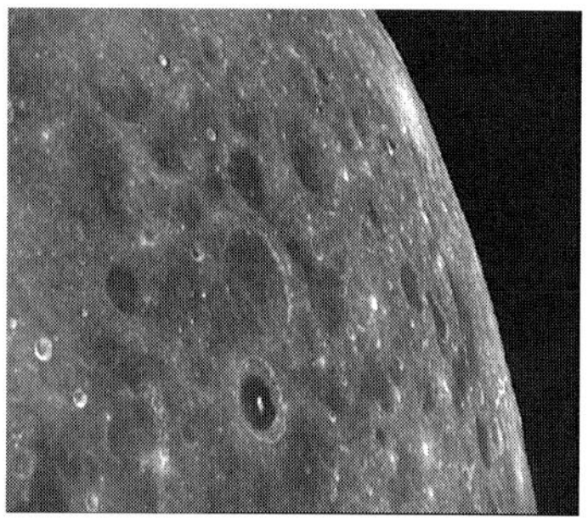

On December 24, *Apollo 8* enters orbit around the moon, and astronauts **Frank Borman**, **Jim Lovell** and **William A. Anders** become the first humans to see the far side of the moon and the Earth as a whole.

For the first time ever, *Time* Magazine features "Men of the Year" instead of "Man of the Year" on its January 1969 cover. *Apollo 8* astronauts Borman, Lovell and Anders take the title as the first men to orbit the moon on the historic flight from December 21–27.

BIRTHS THIS YEAR

Actor Cuba Gooding, Jr.
Rapper LL Cool J
Gymnast Mary Lou Retton
Singer Lisa Marie Presley
Actor Gary Coleman
Actress Lucy Lawless
Singer Céline Dion
Actress Ashley Judd
Terrorist Timothy McVeigh
Actress Traci Lords
Skater Tony Hawk
Singer Kylie Minogue
Actress Debra Messing
Baseball Player Mike Piazza
Actor Will Smith
Actor Hugh Jackman
Baseball Player Sammy Sosa
Actor Owen Wilson

Cuba Gooding, Jr.

Céline Dion

Ashley Judd

Lisa Marie Presley

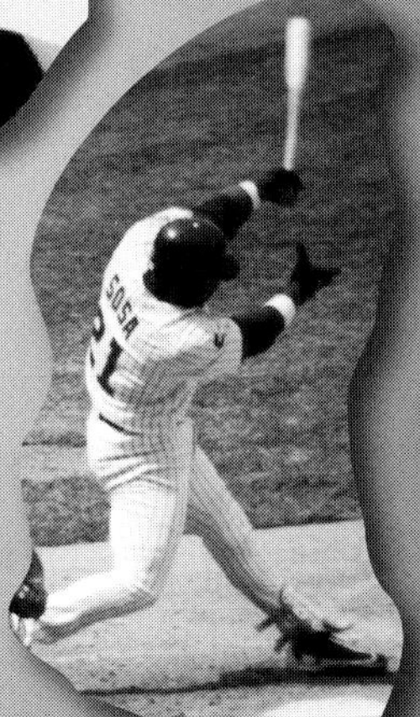

Sammy Sosa

Owen Wilson

Pope Paul VI's encyclical (a letter sent to all the churches in a particular area) Humanae Vitae (Latin for "Of Human Life") reaffirms the Catholic Church's traditional condemnation of birth control. Many expected the Church to reverse its stand on contraception in the wake of the birth control pill, and many Catholic couples ignore the Pope's opinion.

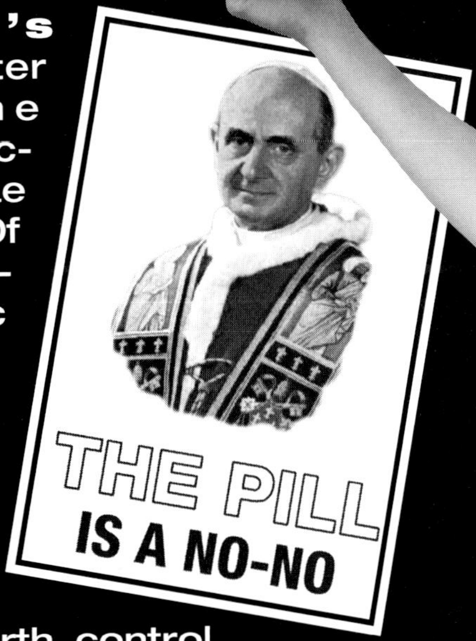

UNBOUGHT AND UNBOSSED WINS THE DAY

Shirley Chisholm is the first African American woman elected to Congress. The Democrat campaigned as an "unbought and unbossed" candidate.

Alec Rose, a 59-year-old yachtsman, completes his singlehanded 28,500-mile sail around the world, arriving on July 4 at Portsmouth, England. Rose, after spending a record 354 days at sea, explains, "It was a boyhood dream. I always felt that the ultimate test of man and ship was to sail around Cape Horn."

Tallulah Bankhead, described by her friends as "tempestuous, tantalizing, talented, an Alabama beauty, aristocrat and actress," dies at age 66.

PASSINGS

Norman M. Thomas, social critic and six-time candidate for President on the Socialist Party ticket, dies at age 84.

•

Actor **Charles Chaplin, Jr.,** age 43, dies after a fall resulting in a blood clot.

•

Edwin O'Connor, novelist and journalist, dies at age 49.

Ulysses S. Grant III dies at age 87.

•

Helen Keller, a deaf-blind activist and author, dies at age 87.

It's No Wonder!

Elizabeth Grossman of North Dakota is chosen **"American Mother of the Year"** by the American Mothers Committee, Inc. Grossman and her husband boast 18 children, 80 grandchildren, and 8 great-grandchildren.

NIXON - AGNEW

Richard Nixon is nominated for U.S. President at the Republican National Convention in Miami Beach, Florida, and chooses **Spiro Agnew** for his vice presidential running mate. In the November presidential election, Nixon defeats Vice President **Hubert Humphrey** and American Independent Party candidate **George C. Wallace**, and pledges that his "first priority foreign policy objective is to bring an honorable end to the war in Vietnam."

Pat Paulsen adds some humor to the 1968 election campaign with his satiric political speeches.

Saundra Williams takes her crown as the first Miss Black America. The 19-year-old singer from Philadelphia says, "With my title, I can show black women that they, too, are beautiful."

Bob Hope accepts the U.S. Military Academy Association of Graduates Sylvanus Thayer Award. "I'm a hawkish dove," he is quoted as saying, "It's nothing like a pigeon, but if I have to lay an egg for my country, I'll do it." Hope is the first entertainer to receive the award "for giving freely of his time and talent to raise the morale and warm the hearts of two generations of servicemen."

Elizabeth Matthew becomes the first woman on the U.S. Military Academy faculty.

Former President Dwight D. Eisenhower celebrates his 78th birthday this year.

Air Force nurse Lt. Jane A. Lombardi is the first woman to receive combat decorations in the Vietnam War.

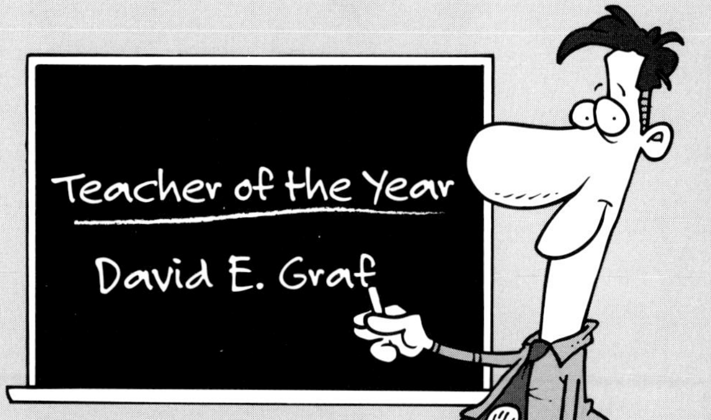

David E. Graf is chosen National Teacher of the Year. The vocational education and industrial arts instructor at a high school in Illinois is cited for "his superior ability to impart knowledge and inspire students with a love of learning." His motto: "Be as firm as you can and be as fair as you can."

According to the Gallup Poll, Americans choose former President **Dwight D. Eisenhower** as the man they most admire for the second year in a row. President **Lyndon B. Johnson** comes in second, and Senator **Edward M. Kennedy** is third. Fourth place goes to the Rev. **Billy Graham**, followed by **Richard M. Nixon, Hubert Humphrey, George Wallace, Pope Paul VI,** former President **Harry S. Truman**, and Senator **Eugene J. McCarthy**.

Wedded Bliss... and Divorce...

Julie Nixon and David Eisenhower both the tender age of 20, wed on December 22. Dr. Norman Vincent Peale performs the ceremony.

Frank Sinatra, 50, had wed Mia Farrow, 21, in a private ceremony at the Sands on July 16, 1966. This year, Sinatra surprises Farrow when he serves her with divorce papers in front of everyone on the set of "Rosemary's Baby."

Wayne Newton, 26, marries former airline stewardess Elaine Okamura at the Flamingo Hotel.

Jacqueline Kennedy and Aristotle Socrates Onassis are married on October 20. The nuptials take place on the island of Skorpios, off the coast of Greece.

Sally Field marries Steven Craig this year, then divorces him in 1975.

and Bizarre!

Franca Viola does NOT wed the man who raped her, angering many in her Sicilian village. Custom dictates that since rape dishonors a woman, she is unfit to wed anyone but her rapist. The 20-year-old, however, flies in the face of tradition by marrying an accountant. Italy's President Saragat witnesses the nuptials.

SORRY I ASKED!?!

Entertainer **Eartha Kitt** speaks out against the Vietnam War at a White House luncheon. Kitt is one of 50 women invited by **Mrs. Lyndon B. Johnson** to discuss urban crime. She surprises the First Lady with her declaration: "You send the best of this country off to be shot and maimed – they rebel in the street."

Dr. Benjamin Spock is indicted on January 5 for his anti-draft advice. Spock says he hopes "100,000, 200,000 or even 500,000 young Americans would refuse to be drafted or obey orders if in the military service."

In the early '50s, Carl Maxie Brashear was the first African American to attend and graduate from the Naval School of Diving and Salvage. Brashear loses his left leg below the knee during an attempt to recover a lost hydrogen bomb off the coast of Palomares, Spain in 1966. During recovery ops, a line used for towing breaks loose and a pipe strikes his leg, nearly shearing it off below the knee. In 1968, after a long recovery and rehabilitation period, Brashear becomes the first amputee to be certified as a diver.

Bruce Reynolds, the last suspect in the Great Train Robbery, is finally arrested after a five-year search in London.

Associate Supreme Court Justice **Abe Fortas** abandons his fight to become Chief Justice to stop what he calls "destructive and extreme assaults upon the court." Fortas had been accused of "lacking judicial propriety" when he accepted a $15,000 lecturer's fee and for continuing to advise President Johnson while serving on the bench.

1968 ADVERTISEMENT

Guess who's behind this glass.

It's______. That's easy to see because new clear rinse Dishwasher Ajax means no spots...just sparkle.

For glasses you can see clear through, for dishes with no spots...just sparkle, use new clear rinse Dishwasher Ajax. Open up your dishwasher and all you see is sparkle. Dishes and glasses so clean and bright they look almost like new. Pretty enough to be in pictures. Put new clear rinse Dishwasher Ajax to work in your automatic and it's no spots...just sparkle.

(The face behind the glass is Jean Harlow, of course.)

Human Interest

According to the Chinese calendar, this is the Year of the Monkey. Those lucky enough to be born in this year are imbued with many positive qualities. They are imaginative, ingenious, resourceful, versatile, persuasive, and have a good sense of humor. On the negative side, they tend to be restless, sly, mischievous, and superficial.

Just The Facts, Ma'am

World Population: 3.556 billion

U.S. Population: 200,706,052

U.S. President: Lyndon B. Johnson

U.S. Vice President: Hubert H. Humphrey

Life Expectancy: 70.2 years

U.S. Violent Crime Rate: 33.7 per 1,000

U.S. Property Crime Rate: 30.7 per 1,000

U.S. Homicide Rate: 7.3 per 100,000

U.S. Population with Religious Affiliation: 128,000,000

Ad Slogans of the Day

Sony Trinitron: "The new color portable that won't give you a hernia"

Eve: **"Farewell to the ugly cigarette."**

Sara Lee Devil's Food Cake: **"The Temptation of Brother Domenico"**

RN Magazine: **"The sexual revolution is spreading a lot more than love."**

Johnny Walker Black: "Honor thy self"

Ohrbach's: **"Will the cost of living going up stop your hemline from coming down?"**

Joan Crawford

Famous people born under the sign of the Monkey include:

Gillian Anderson
Martina Navratilova
Omar Shariff
Caesar

Bob Marley

James Stewart

In reaction to the assassinations of both Martin Luther King, Jr. and Robert Kennedy, Sears & Roebuck removes toy guns from its Christmas catalog and orders all its stores to stop advertising them.

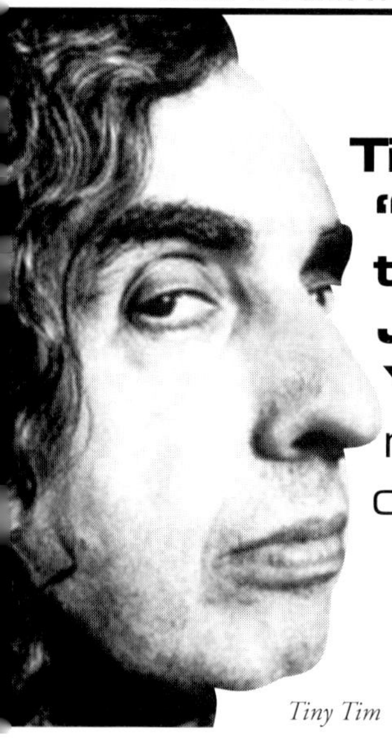
Tiny Tim

Tiny Tim sings **"Tiptoe Through the Tulips,"** and **John Lennon** and **Yoko Ono's** nude record album cover is banned.

Let's Hear It for Long Weekends!

Washington's Birthday, Memorial Day, Columbus Day, and Veteran's Day are all shifted to Monday celebrations.

Higher Education?

The president of San Francisco State University resigns when African American instructors encourage African American students to bring guns onto campus.

• • •

Yale College finally goes coed.

• • •

Ringling Brothers and Barnum & Bailey Clown College in Venice, Florida, becomes the first professional school for training circus clowns.

A World Record AND A Good Deed

For 85 hours, George Hood pedals his stationary bike toward a title in the Guinness Book of World Records and raises $25,000 for COPS, an organization helping families of slain police officers.

°The "Seven Sisters Oak," with a girth of over 38 feet, is made president of the Louisiana Live Oak Society. "Seven Sisters Oak" is located on the shore of Lake Pontchartrain, and is estimated to be about 1,200 years old!

FBI TEN MOST WANTED FUGITIVES

Ruth Eisemann-Schier has the Dubious Distinction of becoming the first woman on the FBI's "Ten Most Wanted" list. Eisemann-Schier will eventually be indicted on Georgia state charges of kidnapping with ransom.

This year a record 32 fugitives are added to list and there are second (Schier's partner, **Gary Steven Krist**) and third (**James Earl Ray**) "Special Additions," which temporarily bring the total most wanted Fugitive count to eleven.

The Age of Protest

In one of the most publicized protests of the '60s, Columbia University students take over five buildings (including the office of President Grayson Kirk) and hold three hostages including Acting Dean Henry Coleman. The protest addresses two issues: the university's ties to the Institute for Defense Analysis; and the proposed building of a university gym in an adjacent black neighborhood, seen as a "racist symbol of Columbia's disregard for black neighborhoods." Five thousand students take part in the demonstrations led by Mark Rudd, president of Students for a Democratic Society, better known as SDS. In the end, 700 are arrested and 148 are hurt.

Chicago police are criticized for attacks on demonstrators at the Democratic National Convention. Although a presidential panel concludes that protestors did provoke police with "obscene epithets, and of rocks, sticks, bathroom tiles and even human feces," it also accuses the police of having responded with "unrestrained and indiscriminate police violence on many occasions, particularly at night." Famous protestors in attendance at Chicago's Democratic Convention include Abbie Hoffman and Jerry Rubin (Youth International Party), Tom Hayden (SDS) and Bobby Seale (Black Panther Party).

The President's National Advisory Commission on Civil Disorders states that the U.S. is "moving toward two societies, one black, one white, separate and unequal." The report ties widespread rioting to "white racism" and urges bans on discriminatory practices.

A civil rights protest staged at a white-only bowling alley in Orangeburg, South Carolina is broken up by highway patrolmen, leading to the deaths of three college students.

On May 17, the Catonsville Nine (nine Catholics) go to the draft board in Catonsville, Maryland, take 378 draft files to the parking lot in wire baskets, pour homemade napalm over them, and set them on fire. This dramatic protest against the Vietnam War ends in federal court in October, where the nine are found guilty of destruction of U.S. property, destruction of Selective Service files, and interference with the Selective Service Act of 1967.

When Judith Malina and Julian Beck's Living Theatre Group tours "Paradise Now," which protests drug laws and clothing, they are arrested 15 times.

Feminists picket the Miss America contest, trashing girdles and bras.

Notable Quotables

American novelist **William Burroughs** declares: "The youth rebellion is a worldwide phenomenon that has not been seen before in history. I do not believe they will calm down and be ad execs at thirty as the Establishment would like us to believe."

Feminist leader **Betty Friedan**: "No girl child born today should responsibly be brought up to be a housewife. Too much has been made of defining human personality and destiny in terms of the sex organs. After all, we share the human brain."

• • • • •

Martin Luther King, Jr., along with the Southern Christian Leadership Conference, organizes the "Poor People's Campaign" to address economic injustice. The march begins in Mississippi, crossing the U.S. to assemble what King calls "a multiracial army of the poor." The march ends in Washington, D.C. on May 12, with protestors demanding that Congress enact a poor people's bill of rights. Unfortunately, the campaign ends in mid-June without passing the hoped-for economic bill of rights.

• • • • •

Pretty Postage

Legislation passes allowing postage stamps to be illustrated in color.

• • • • •

In Moscow, Aeroflot and Pan Am open direct service between the U.S. and the Soviet Union.

• • • • •

Jamaican Sislin Fay Allen becomes Britain's first black policewoman.

The **Beatles** shut down all their business in the USA, turning it all over to **Apple Records**.

• • • • •

The Medal of Honor is posthumously awarded to James Anderson, Jr. - the first African American U.S. Marine to receive this award.

• • • • •

SIXTY-SEVEN-YEAR-OLD LOUIS ARMSTRONG BECOMES THE OLDEST PERSON TO HAVE A NUMBER ONE HIT WITH "WHAT A WONDERFUL WORLD."

• • • • •

January 1, 1968: Evel Knievel crashes in an attempt to clear the fountains at Caesar's Palace in Las Vegas.

• • • • •

Michigan is the first state to repeal its helmet law, beginning a pattern of repeal, reenactment, and amendment.

1968 IS THE YEAR THE UNITED STATES' POPULATION TOPS THE 200,000,000 MARK.

Across The Pond...

Top English Ads

1. Oxo
2. The Milk Marketing Board
3. Weetabix
4. Heinz soups
5. The Daily Mirror
6. Vim scouring cleaner
7. Mackintosh's Quality Street
8. Daz washing powder
9. Stork margarine
10. Ambrosia milk pudding
11. Maxwell House coffee
12. Galaxy milk chocolate
13. Rowntrees' After Eight mints
14. Guinness
15. McVitie and Price digestive biscuits

The Engine That Could

The last steam passenger train service runs in Britain. The locomotive makes its 120-mile journey from Liverpool to Carlisle and back before its last trip to the wrecking yard.

The Bridge That Couldn't

Unable to support the weight of modern-day traffic, the London Bridge is sold to an American entrepreneur, Robert P. McCulloch, for $2,460,000. The bridge is disassembled and each piece numbered for ease of reassembly, and shipped to Lake Havasu City, Arizona, where the reconstruction begins. Completed and opened in 1971, the bridge spans a man-made river between Lake Havasu and Thompson Bay and is the centerpiece of McCulloch's English-themed village. The bridge was rebuilt using a concrete frame with the actual London Bridge stones used as facing. An urban legend surfaces that McCulloch thought he bought London's more impressive Tower Bridge, but he insists it is just a rumor. Not all of the bridge was sold to McCulloch; a large number of pieces remain in England in lieu of taxes. Originally designed by engineer John Rennie in 1821, the London Bridge is now Arizona's second largest tourist attraction.

TREKKIES UNITE!

When NBC announces the cancellation of *Star Trek*, fans protest from America to Australia. The first Australian Star Trek Fan Club is launched by John Stepkowsi and they start a letter-writing campaign. In America, Caltech students in Southern California protest the rumored cancellation by picketing NBC Studios in Burbank. An unprecedented letter-writing campaign brings a rumored one million letters of protest to NBC. Fans are victorious and NBC renews the show for another season, but it is ultimately canceled in 1969.

In November, a *Star Trek* episode has the first fictional-character interracial kiss to appear on U.S. television. The censors demand that Uhura and Captain Kirk share a closed mouth kiss with "no racial overtones."

In the years since its cancellation, *Star Trek* has become a cultural phenomenon the world over. There is an amazing array of television series, books, movies, and fan events. In fact, *The Guinness Book of World Records* lists *Star Trek* as the television series with the largest number of spin-offs. Even NASA plays a part when, in 1976, they name the Space Shuttle prototype *Enterprise* after receiving 400,000 letters from Trekkies.

"We are at a crisis point in the history of American education and probably in that of the Western world."

Richard Hofstadter, Columbia University professor

The ILLIAC "supercomputer" is built at the University of Illinois, performing an astounding 39 million computations per second.

This year sees a notable increase in college courses dealing with Oriental theology, religion, sorcery, witchcraft, and Zen.

THOSE AMAZING ANIMALS

The last Przewalski's horse, the only truly wild horse whose ancestors were never domesticated, is seen in Mongolia.

Apparently, animal trainer Bob Martwick knew what he was doing when he adopted **"Morris the Cat"** from a Chicago animal shelter. Morris quickly becomes one of the most famous animal stars in the U.S., landing a job as "spokescat" for 9Lives cat food. There will be several Morrises over the years, and all are shelter or rescue cats.

An Exotic Animal Tissue Bank is established at the St. Louis Zoo to preserve tissue from foreign animals for research. By year's end, the bank collects over 1,000 specimens.

The Mongolian gerbil is used in epilepsy research. It seems the poor animal is very susceptible to spontaneous seizures, apparently caused by sudden changes in environment.

Mighty Mouse or Multi-Mouse? A mouse with two fathers and two mothers is born in North Carolina University's Reproductive Physiology Research Lab. This feat is accomplished when a lab tech fuses two fertilized eggs.

British and Russian zoo officials try to mate two giant pandas. Sadly, all attempts fail, leaving China the only country to have bred the giant pandas in captivity.

Aquariums in the U.S. and Canada attract record crowds with killer whale displays. Although fiercely predatory in the wild, killer whales have been taught to exchange kisses with their trainers.

PERPETUALLY POPULAR POT

As more and more people turn to amphetamines to pep up, barbiturates to calm down, and hallucinogens to turn on, marijuana retains its popularity this year. "Pot" finds its way into affluent suburbs, college dorms, and the military, with an estimated 20 million users in the U.S. alone. The American Medical Association and the National Research Council of the National Academy of Sciences conclude that "even weak marijuana preparations can cause antisocial behavior with serious consequences." The federal government finally gets into the act, and on April 18, the Bureau of Narcotics and the Bureau of Drug Abuse Control combine to form the new Bureau of Narcotics and Dangerous Drugs. Congress stiffens penalties for illegal manufacture and sale of hallucinogenic drugs, making illegal possession a misdemeanor punishable by a $1,000 fine or up to one year in prison or both for the first and second offenses, with a $10,000 fine or up to three years in prison or both for subsequent offenses.

IAN MCLAGAN OF THE MUSICAL GROUP THE SMALL FACES IS ARRESTED AT HEATHROW AIRPORT FOR CARRYING CANNABIS.

"Monkee" Mickey Dolenz marries English model and *Top of the Pops* presenter **Samantha Juste.**

Theirs was a whirlwind romance. When asked about the first time they met, Dolenz says: "I saw her sitting in the TV canteen drinking tea. I thought she was attractive. I didn't know she was a model or that she had anything to do with the show. Later I saw her putting on the records for Jimmy Saville, the deejay of *Tops*. Mike Nesmith and I were appearing on the show to be awarded an English Gold Disc for 'I'm a Believer.' Cyril Black, a London Screen Gems rep, was with me when I told him I thought 'that girl' was cute and he said he knew her. He called her up and introduced us. I wanted to ask her to have dinner with me, but I was afraid she'd say no. Anyway, I got up my nerve – and she said YES! We went to Bag O' Nails for dinner and then we went dancing. That was the beginning..."

Jamaican-born athlete **Bob Beamon** sets a world record for the long jump at the 1968 Mexico City Summer Olympics. His record of 29 feet, 2 1/2 inches will stand for 23 years!

• • • • •

Swissair's slogan: "Don't Go Home With Strangers."

• • • • •

BBC's Radio Nottingham launches the first phone-in program entitled *What Are They Up To Now?*

• • • • •

Martha Vasconcellos is Brazil's second Miss Universe, while runner-up **Anne Marie Braafheid** of Curaçao becomes the highest placing black delegate in Miss Universe history.

• • • • •

Heroin addiction increases by about 10 times over the past 15 years, with the number of registered addicts reaching over 2,700.

• • • • •

The "Giant New Year's Eve Gala Pop and Blues Party" takes place at Alexandra Palace.

• • • • •

British pop singer **Sandie Shaw** marries fashion designer **Jeff Banks**.

In July, Decca Records in England and London Records refuse to release ***Beggars Banquet*** by the **Rolling Stones** because of its planned cover, a graffiti-covered lavatory. In response, the band holds back the album and **Mick Jagger** says, "I don't find the cover we proposed at all offensive. Decca has put out a sleeve showing an atom bomb exploding. I find that more upsetting."

By November the Rolling Stones concede and the album is released in December with a simple imitation invitation card cover.

On his 21st birthday, Peter Noone of Herman's Hermits fame marries 22-year-old French beauty Mireille Strasser.

Rolling Stone Brian Jones is arrested for the second time for possession of marijuana.

WHERE'S RINGO?

Ringo Starr walks out on the Beatles while recording The White Album, claiming he is "disgusted with the band's tensions and bored waiting around to contribute." Starr spends the next two weeks on **Peter Sellers'** yacht writing "Octopus's Garden" before his return. When he does return, he finds his drum kit covered with flowers.

Exotic love potions for the bath and afterbath.

KiKU – like love – smooths the body,
soothes the soul, embraces your whole being
with long-lingering, spirt-sparkling
scent. In gleaming yellow and golden
treasure boxes for gifting and getting.
Shamelessly feminine, Fabulously Fabergé!

KIKU BATH EXOTICS: After Bath Cologne, Bath Oil, Bath Powder, Bath Soap, Bath Brush, Bodysoft.

Disasters

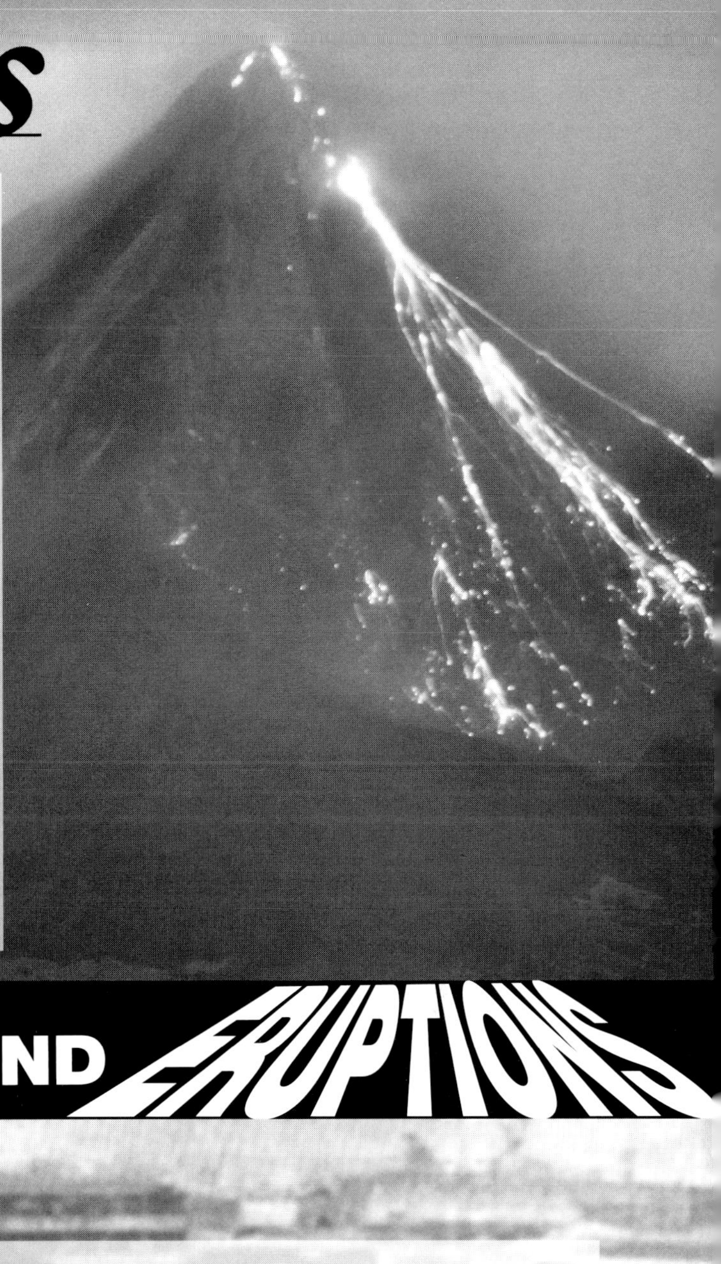

Costa Rica's Mount Arenal, quiet for almost five centuries, erupts this year. Volcanic ash spreads for miles, as much as 3 feet deep in places. At least 78 people die, and 10 searchers for the missing are engulfed in flames and incinerated. Nearby Nicaragua, El Salvador, and Mexico offer aid, and U.S. C-130 transports help deliver relief supplies to nearly 5,000 evacuees. The effect on Costa Rica's cattle industry is catastrophic. Eight hundred head of cattle die in the eruption, 80,000 are ordered slaughtered for immediate sale, and a further 100,000 are moved to new pasture lands. By the end of the week, Arenal is rumbling ominously again and a team of volcanologists arrive from Washington, hoping to find the reason for the eruption and hopefully to figure out how to predict further eruptions.

EARTHQUAKES AND ERUPTIONS

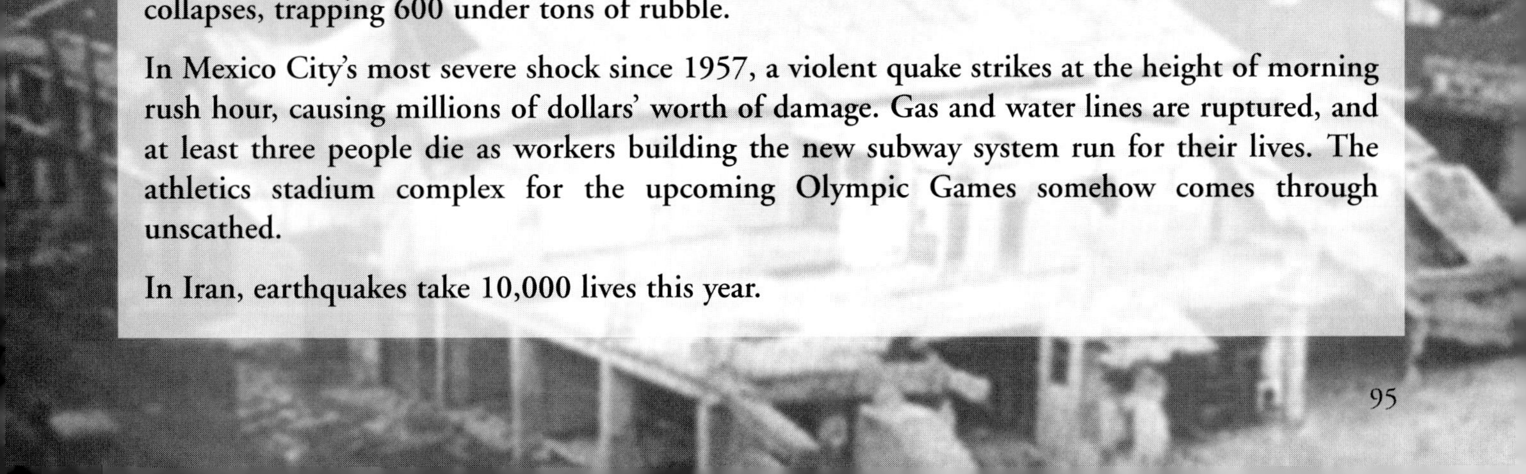

In the Philippines' worst earthquake in a decade, 111 are killed during the one-minute predawn shaker that catches most people still in bed. Glass panes are blown out of the airport control tower, and the Ruby Towers, a five-story apartment building in Manila's Chinese quarter, collapses, trapping 600 under tons of rubble.

In Mexico City's most severe shock since 1957, a violent quake strikes at the height of morning rush hour, causing millions of dollars' worth of damage. Gas and water lines are ruptured, and at least three people die as workers building the new subway system run for their lives. The athletics stadium complex for the upcoming Olympic Games somehow comes through unscathed.

In Iran, earthquakes take 10,000 lives this year.

Waiting For Rain

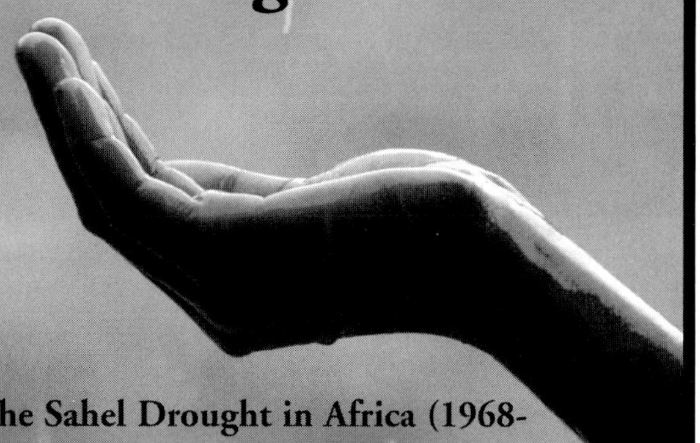

The Sahel Drought in Africa (1968-1974) is perhaps the most devastating in recent history. Between 50,000 and 100,000 people perish, nearly 5.5 million are displaced, and the agricultural bases of Ethiopia, Sudan, Mali, Niger, and Chad crumble.

Researcher Camilla Toulmin writes that in addition to "livestock losses and post-drought rehabilitation in sub-Saharan Africa, the Sahelian region also suffered extensive damage to cattle, sheep and goats, losing between 15-45% of each group." The national governments of this region lose nearly 3% of their tax revenue, and approximately half the individuals in the region flee their rural communities to more developed urban centers.

Coal Mine Disaster

November 20 sees the first major mining disaster of the television age. Seventy-eight coal miners die when they are trapped by explosions in a mine in Farmington, West Virginia. As big as Manhattan, the mine is just several miles from Monongah, which, in 1907, was the site of the worst mine disaster in U.S. history. The explosion rips through the mine at 5:30 a.m. and is so huge that a motel clerk 12 miles away thought the rear of the motel had exploded. Within hours, 21 miners reach the surface, but 78 remain missing. By the 29th, rescuers accept defeat as readings of underground gases prove the air is unable to sustain life, and all entrances to the mine are sealed. Attempts to recover the missing miners' bodies continue for 10 years, but in the end 59 are brought to the surface and 19 remain entombed. Although the source of the explosion is never determined, investigators do find inadequacies in ventilation, control of explosive methane gas, and testing for methane. This disaster proves to be the catalyst for the 1969 Coal Mine Safety and Health Act, strengthening safety standards, increasing inspections, and providing specific safety and health rights to coal miners, basically making the coal mines of the United States safer places to work.

Avalanches in Switzerland and Southwest Poland claim over 40 lives.

In March, 6,249 sheep become ill in Skull Valley, Utah, about 30 miles from the Dugway chemical testing site. The sheep are found to have been poisoned by an organophosphate chemical, possibly a pesticide. Although there had been local tests of a nerve agent, the Army does not admit liability but does pay the ranchers for their losses. The official record shows a claim for 4,372 disabled sheep plus costs for another 1,877 sheep that were permanently injured or potentially exposed.

MARITIME MYSTERY

Shortly before midnight on May 16, the **USS *Scorpion*** reportedly receives a top-secret message to change course and head for the Canary Islands toward a mysterious collection of Soviet ships. In its last reported sighting, the sub surfaces in Spain to release 2 men with emergency leave orders. The sub is last heard from on May 21, south of the Azores, and six days later is reported overdue at Norfolk, Virginia. Five months later, its wreckage is found 2 miles down on the ocean floor about 400 nautical miles southwest of the Azores. All 99 men aboard are dead.

Evidence suggests that the boat, which contained highly sophisticated spy gear and spy manuals, 2 nuclear-tipped torpedoes, and a nuclear propulsion system, sank on May 22 after an explosion. Some argue there was no explosion, and suggest hostile action by a Soviet sub. The Navy's conclusions, printed in 1968, are classified and conclude that "no one is likely ever to conclusively determine the cause for the loss." Navy spokesman **Commander Frank Thorp** reports: "While the precise cause of the loss remains undetermined, there is no information to support the theory that the submarine's loss resulted from hostile action or any involvement by a Soviet ship or submarine."

A rumor surfaces that **John Walker**, the Navy's most notorious spy, gave codes to the Soviets to track the sub. Some Russian admirals state that U.S. and Soviet officials agreed to cover up the incident to avoid damaging relations between the two countries. Commander Thorp declines to comment on the Walker connection, and the cause of the disaster remains a mystery.

Naples, Italy on April 10, 1968: The *Scorpion's* line handling crew just after she has been made fast alongside the *Tallahatchie County*.

The *Scorpion* (SSN-589) is put into the water at the Gen-eral Dynamics Corp.'s Electric Boat Division in Groton, Connecticut on December 19, 1959.

Shortly before departure on her last voyage, the *Scorpion* comes alongside the *Tallahatchie County* (AVB-2) outside of Claywall Harbor in Naples, Italy. April 10, 1968.

The Hong Kong Flu pandemic of 1968-1969 kills over 750,000 people worldwide.

An explosion and fire at the Mickelberry's Food Products plant in Chicago kills the president of the company and eight others, including a fire department captain and four firemen.

Seven days of floods in India take 1,000 lives.

When turnstiles slow the exit of 90,000 fans from El Estadio Monumental soccer stadium in Buenos Aires, 70 people are killed in the ensuing stampede.

On January 28, a U.S. Air Force B-52 bomber crashes while attempting an emergency landing in Greenland. The Defense Department says the four hydrogen bombs on board are "unarmed so that there is no danger of a nuclear explosion at the crash site." A co-pilot is killed, but the remaining six crew members parachute to safety. The plane was on an airborne alert (by the Strategic Air Command) to protect its bombers from a surprise missile attack.

Hurricane Abby brings heavy rains to the Florida Keys, killing seven.

The ferry boat *Wahine* capsizes and sinks off Wellington Harbour in New Zealand with over 700 people on board. Though badly damaged from running aground on a reef, the powerless vessel drifts into the harbor waters, and all but 51 are rescued.

The ferry boat *Dumaguete* sinks in the Sulu Sea strait off Mindanao in the Philippines. Only 18 survive of the estimated 3,500 passengers.

When the British steamer *Eastern Moon* rams into the motorboat *Iruna*, only 37 of the 200 passengers survive.

Just an hour from her base, the French submarine *Minerve* disappears in the Mediterranean with 52 aboard.

The oil service ship *Triple Crown* capsizes and sinks off the coast of Santa Barbara, California.

AN OUNCE OF PREVENTION, A POUND OF CURE...

UNESCO's (United Nations Educational, Scientific and Cultural Organization) Intergovernmental Oceanographic Commission (IOC) launches a successful International Tsunami Warning System for the Pacific, the only one in the world.

Congress creates the National Flood Insurance Program (NFIP) to stem the rising cost of taxpayer-funded flood disaster relief and the rising amount of damage caused by floods. The National Flood Insurance Act offers new flood protection to homeowners.

What's New

1968 ADVERTISEMENT

WORLD'S FIRST* 500 CC DUAL-STROKE

*POSI-FORCE

SUZUKI 500/FIVE

New Products and Inventions

The first Big Mac and the first Hot Apple Pie go on sale at McDonald's.

Don Wetzel says he conceived the idea of the automated teller machine (ATM) while waiting in line at a Dallas bank. Wetzel, a vice president of Docutel (the company that developed automated baggage-handling equipment), co-patented the ATM with two engineers, Tom Barnes and George Chastain. The working prototype came about a year later, and the first ATM is installed in a New York bank in 1973.

A LEFTY'S LIFE MADE EASIER

"**Anything Left Handed**" begins to make left-handed products and provide information for left-handers.

☆ ☆ ☆

"Estée" is the second fragrance created by Estée Lauder.

☆ ☆ ☆

The emergency **911** telephone service is born in the United States. Manned 24 hours a day, 365 days a year, it provides one phone number for reporting emergencies.

☆ ☆ ☆

President Lyndon B. Johnson watches as the Lockheed **C-5 Galaxy**, the world's largest plane, rolls off the assembly line on March 2. The Galaxy is a military transport designed to carry oversized cargo, and is used exclusively by the U.S. Air Force. On June 30, the Lockheed-Georgia Co. begins flight-testing the Galaxy under the call sign "Allen-zero-three-heavy."

When David Blechman, a worker in the pharmaceutical industry, has an idea for a liquid protein product, he and his wife, Jean, quit their jobs to start Twin Laboratories. Named for their two sets of twins, Twinlab Corporation's mission *"is to be the best-in-class nutritional and wellness company delivering high quality, innovative products and services globally."* Ultimately, the company will manufacture vitamins, minerals, and bodybuilding supplements.

1968 ADVERTISEMENT

Philip Morris introduces new 100mm Virginia Slims, and the ads feature slender women wearing the latest fashions. The slogan "You've Come a Long Way" doesn't include the word "baby" yet. Meanwhile, Reynolds' Doral cigarette represents the low-cost, generic end of the cigarette business.

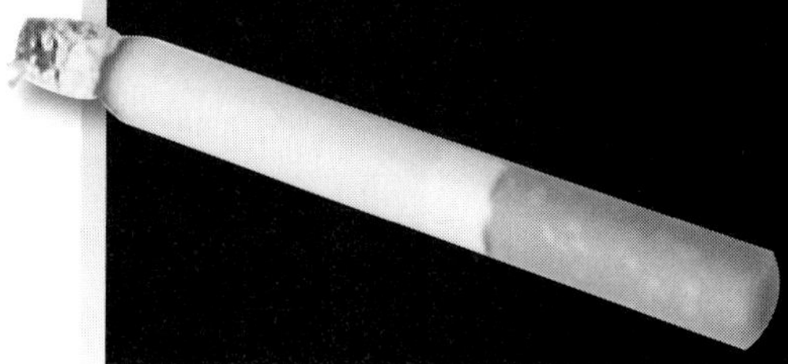

Nobody Doesn't Like Sara Lee!

Mitch Leigh, composer of the Broadway musical *Man of La Mancha,* writes "Nobody Doesn't Like Sara Lee." The jingle becomes the core of all the company's new ads, even appearing on all of Sara Lee's trucks.

Corning Glass Works

Corning introduces "Pyrex Store 'N' See ware." They also introduce the "Counter-that-Cooks" electric range. Under its smooth glass surface are four invisible heating elements, and it comes with a set of "Cookmates," special pots with ground and polished bottoms for perfect contact with the heat source.

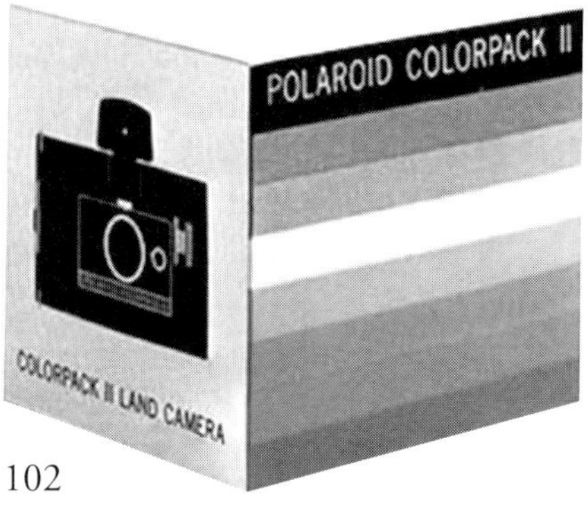

The first color striped package design hits the stores with Polaroid color film. Advertising vice president Peter Wensberg insists on the colorful box to appeal to shoppers and look good on TV.

AUTO INNOVATIONS

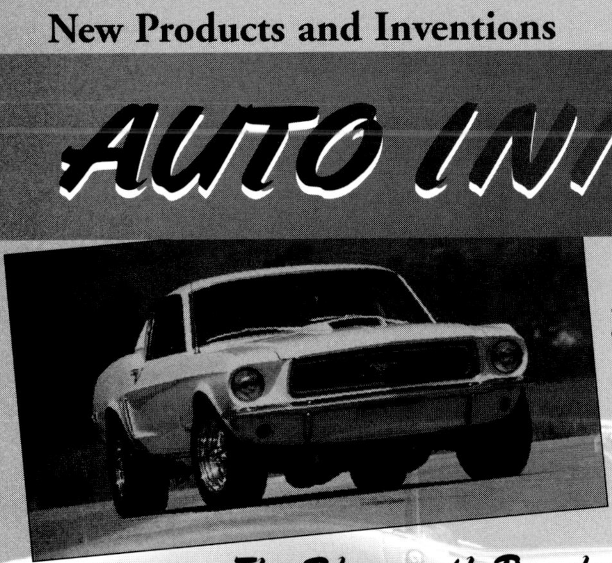

The Ford Mustang gets a new grille, chrome trim, and a thinner "corral" around the pony!

The Plymouth Roadrunner lacks the chrome, fancy bucket seats, and carpets of the '60s "muscle cars" and enters the market as a stripped-down, inexpensive, "no frills, high thrills" performer!

The Corolla is the smallest car Toyota had ever offered in the United States, and sells for a mere $1,700.

The Corvette undergoes a controversial restyle. Reviews are mixed, but car aficionados buy 28,566 this year alone!

Shoulder harnesses on seat belts are introduced.

Over three billion Hot Wheels cars have been produced since their birth in 1968 — more than the total production of Detroit's "Big Three" auto makers combined!

Boys and Their Toys

Yellow Submarine

The Beatles' movie *Yellow Submarine* has kids everywhere playing with their own yellow subs.

The **Batman Utility Belt**, a "complete set of crime fighting equipment," includes handcuffs and a super gun!

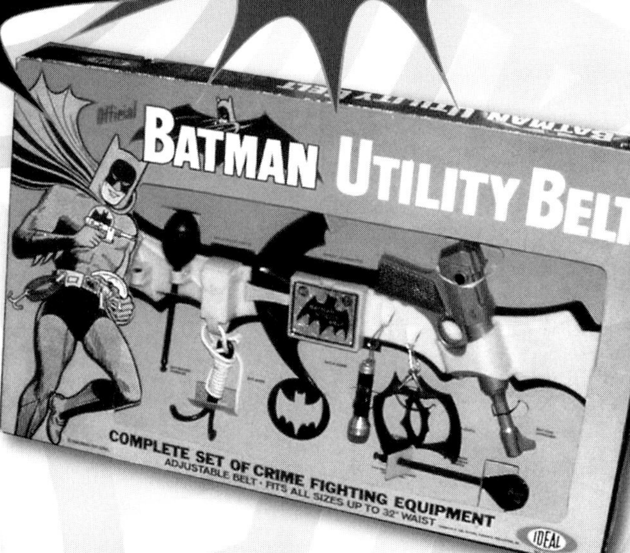

Snoopy Scores

Fisher-Price scores in a big way with their Snoopy "dog on wheels." Snoopy barks after every step as toddlers pull him along by his little plastic lead.

Do You Remember?

Hasbro introduces ***The Kooky Spookys*** finger puppets. This funny family of ghosts include Daddy Booregard, Baby Spook 'em, Teena Terror, Brother Mortimer, and Grandma Macreak.

Colorforms comes out with ***Outer Space Men***, three-dimensional bendable extraterrestrials such as Commander Comet, Astro-Nautilus, Electron +, Alpha 7, Xodiac, Orbitron, and Colossus Rex.

Barbie begins to talk. but her words are making feminists fume with phrases like "Math class is hard" and "Help me with my hair." Mattel introduces Barbie's friend ***Christie***, their first African American doll with ethnic features.

Mattel's ***Battling Tops*** action game consists of 2 to 4 players facing off in an arena, each with his or her own spinning top. The last player spinning wins, and the first to win 10 rounds is the grand champion!

U.S. Games Systems (USGS), founded this year by Stuart R. Kaplan, initially markets only tarot cards. Eventually, the company will produce playing cards, games, books, and specialty advertising products.

The first 747-100 rolls out of the factory in September.

A REAL LIFESAVER

The **Skadi**, the first effective electronic avalanche rescue beacon (radio transceiver), is created by a research team headed by **John Lawton** at Cornell Aëronautical Laboratory in Buffalo, New York. Earlier efforts lacked the range and accuracy needed to save lives. Several years later, the Skadi will become a standard item for ski patrollers.

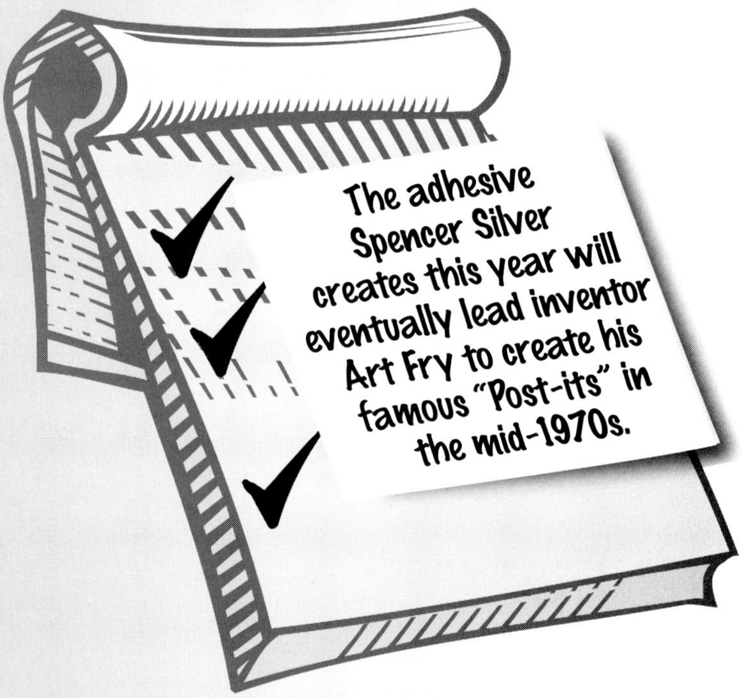

Kodel polyester fabric and the beanbag make a big hit in '68!

COMPUTER CONCEPTIONS

Dr. Robert Dennard patents DRAM (dynamic random access memory), which in layman's terms is a "type of computer memory that can be accessed randomly and quickly."

A MOUSE BY ANY OTHER NAME?

The "x-y position indicator"

Douglas Engelbart

The computer mouse is demonstrated by its creator Douglas Engelbart this year. It is made with wood encasing two metal wheels. He originally calls it an "x-y position indicator," although its nickname is the "Mouse" because the "tail" comes out the end.

HP introduces the 9100, its first desktop programmable calculator with computer-like capabilities. Built without any integrated circuits, it has a CRT display, printed circuit board ROM, and a magnetic core memory. Costing around $4,900.00 and weighing just 40 pounds, it is now considered to be the forerunner of the personal computer.

Powerful Computing Genie: $4900

READY, WILLING AND ABLE.

Ready—to relieve you of waiting to get on the big computer. Constantly available. At your fingertips whenever you need it. Ready to abolish tedium from scientific and engineering computation. Ready to slash through long routines and come up with answers in milliseconds. *The new Hewlett-Packard 9100A personal computer.*

Willing—to perform log and trig functions, even hyperbolics and coordinate transformations, at the touch of a key. Willing to work with extremely large and small numbers simultaneously. Willing to take your programming commands in mathematical language. No computer language or programming specialist required. Willing to communicate with you on *your* terms. *The new Hewlett-Packard 9100A computing marvel.*

Able—to take on the most complex problems: roots of a fifth-degree polynomial . . . solutions to three simultaneous equations . . . Bessel functions . . . Fourier analysis . . . elliptic integrals . . . real and complex polynomial evaluation . . . coordinate geometry . . . regression analysis . . . numerical integration . . . vector analysis . . . and many, many more! Able to be your fast, responsive mathematical servant. *The new Hewlett-Packard 9100A electronic genie.*

This major computing capability is compressed into one 40 pound package. Its only moving parts are the keys, the switches and one decimal wheel. No noise.

The 9100A computing genie is being delivered *NOW*, with an extensive—and growing—program library that puts you in control.

Examine the keyboard, question every key and switch. Then decide to command the computing genie. A telephone call or purchase order directed to any HP Sales and Service Office (in principal cities throughout the world) will start the executive process. If you are still skeptical, or of faint heart ask for a demonstration. It will affirm, assure (and only slightly delay) your entry into the solid-state of personal computing power. Be a Master. Hewlett-Packard, Box 301, Loveland, Colorado, 80537; Europe: 54 Route des Acacias, Geneva.

9100A puts answers just a touch away!

HEWLETT hp PACKARD

Dynamic range 10^{-99} to 10^{99}, nearly 200 decades. Observation of math operations on 3 displayed registers. Up to 16 more registers for data storage.

Complex and vector arithmetic simplified with coordinate transformation keys, rectangular-to-polar and vice-versa, in milliseconds.

Trig functions covering all quadrants and any size angle in degrees or radians.

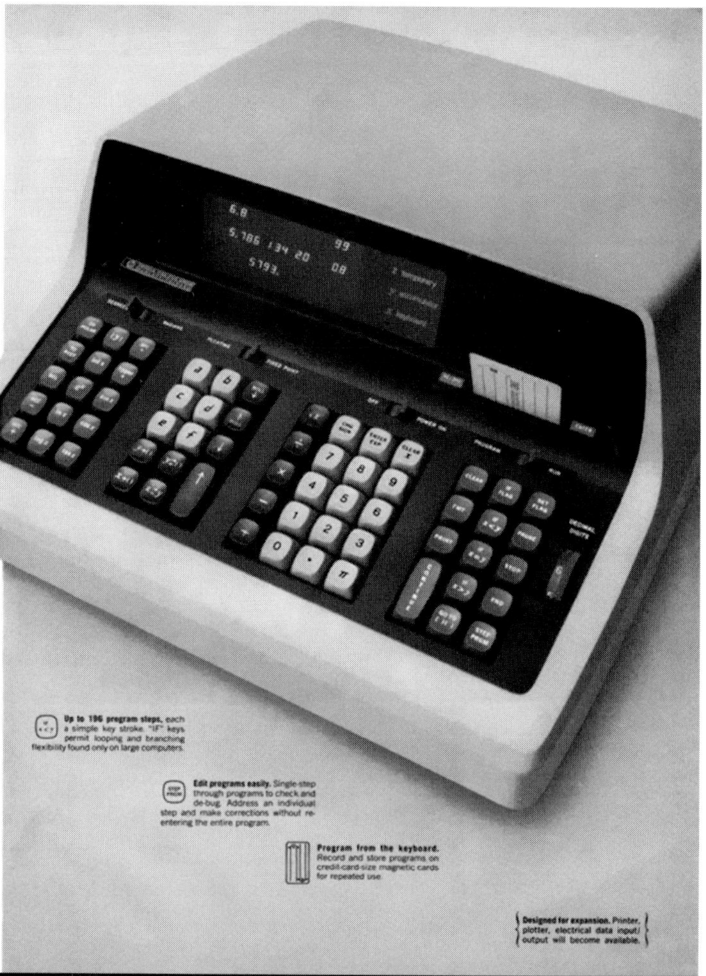

The New Emancipator

63 KEYS TO COMPUTING FREEDOM ARE NOW WITHIN YOUR REACH!

Freedom from waiting to get on the BIG computer.

Freedom from translating your problems into foreign computer languages.

Freedom from starvation-level computing with under-developed calculators.

Freedom from the drudgery of manual computation.

The new hp 9100A puts heroic computing power responsively at your fingertips . . . for the unheroic, one-time-cost of $4900. Fast core memory delivers answers to log, trig and other keystroke functions in milliseconds. And . . . in seconds you get answers to more complex computations such as roots of a fifth degree polynomial . . . Fourier analysis . . . elliptic integrals . . . Fresnel integrals . . . real and complex polynomial evaluation . . . coordinate geometry . . . regression analysis . . . three dimensional vectors . . . numerical integration and many, many, more!

This major computing capability is compressed into one 40 pound package. Its only moving parts are the keys, the switches and one decimal wheel. No noise!

The 9100A is being delivered now along with an extensive – and growing – program library that puts you in control.

Examine the keyboard. Question every key and switch. Then join the participators! A telephone call or purchase order directed to any Hewlett-Packard sales and service office (located in principal cities throughout the world) will start your liberation from the tyranny and tradition of too BIG, too slow and too weak. If you are still skeptical or of faint heart, ask for a demonstration. It will affirm, assure and delay – but only slightly – your entry into the solid-state of personal computing freedom. Hurry. Being a leader has its advantages. Hewlett-Packard, P.O. Box 301, Loveland, Colorado 80537. Europe: 54 Route des Acacias, Geneva.

9100A puts answers just a touch away!

HEWLETT hp PACKARD

Dynamic range 10^{-99} to 10^{99}, nearly 200 decades. Observation of math operations on 3 displayed registers. Up to 16 more registers for data storage.

Complex and vector arithmetic simplified with coordinate transformation keys, rectangular-to-polar and vice-versa, in milliseconds.

Trig functions covering all quadrants and any size angle in degrees or radians.

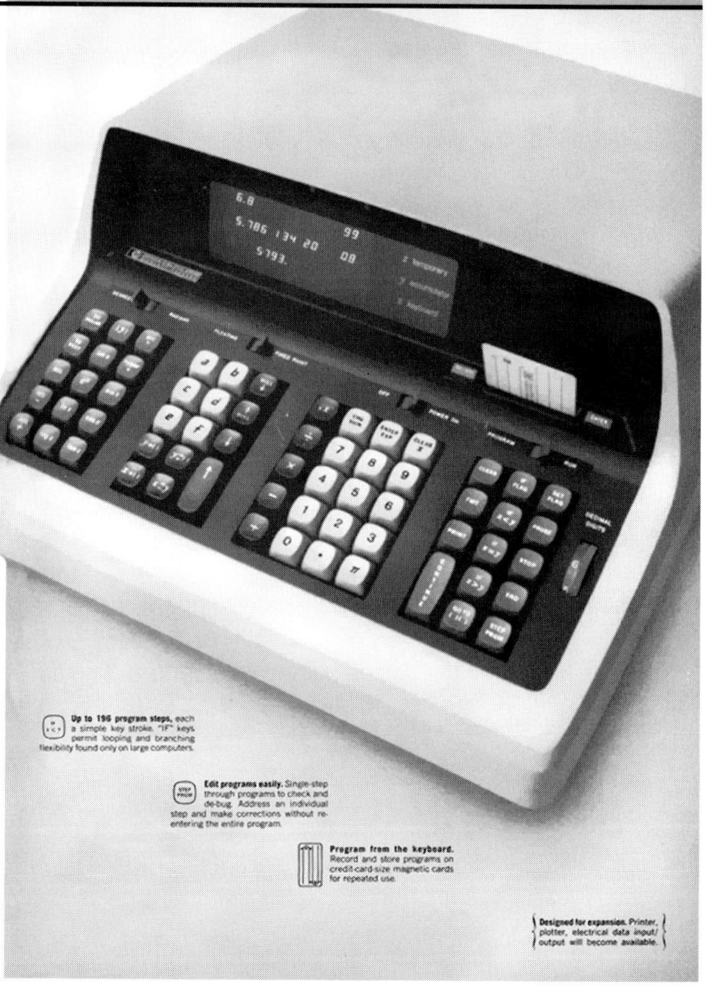

Food News

Soul Food

becomes fashionable fare this year. The April issue of *Esquire* declares: "Soul food is why it is chic to have a soul sister in the kitchen." Craig Claiborne, restaurant critic, food writer, and food editor of the *New York Times,* says, "New York's soul food restaurants – and they are increasing – are discussed with enthusiasm at sophisticated cocktail gatherings."

Since many white middle- and upper-class Americans are having a hard time with chitlins (small intestines of pigs), not to mention pigs' feet, pigs' tails, and possum, many soul food restaurants catering to whites drop these items from their menus.

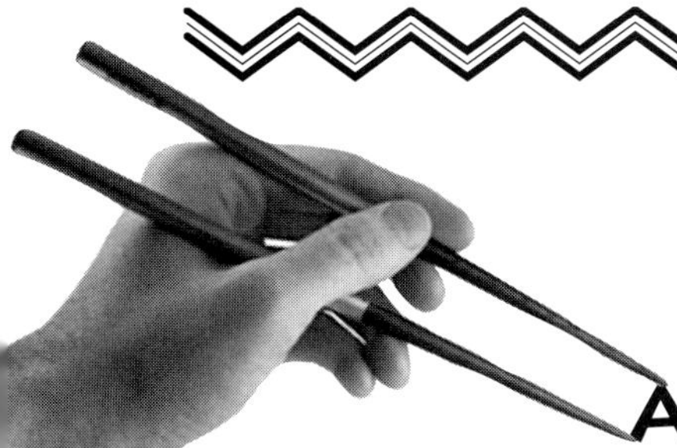

ALTHOUGH CHINESE RESTAURANTS STILL LEAD THE PACK FOR ETHNIC FARE, TASTES ARE CHANGING AND JAPANESE, VIETNAMESE, AND THAI FOODS ARE ALSO BECOMING POPULAR.

The Taco Salad

The Taco Salad is a modern version of a "Tex-Mex" dish and is a favorite this year.

According to Jean Anderson, American Century Cookbook: *The Most Popular Recipes of the 20th Century,* "This salad arrived with the Tex-Mex fast-food franchises, which began to pepper the country in the 60s. The man who whetted our appetite for 'hot and spicy' was Glen Bell, who opened the first Taco Bell in Downey, California in 1962. Did Taco Bell originate the Taco Salad? I've been unable to prove it did. Or didn't. The first recipe I could find for Taco Salad appeared in the May 1968 issue of *Sunset.*"

Sunset Magazine recipe for Taco Salad
May 1968

1 lb lean ground beef
1/4 c. finely chopped onion
1/2 tsp salt
2 tsp chili powder
1 can (8oz) tomato sauce
1 medium head iceberg lettuce
1/2 c. shredded cheddar cheese
2 medium-sized tomatoes, peeled and cut in wedges
1 avocado, peeled and sliced
1-1/2 c. corn chips or tortilla chips

Fry meat and onion over medium-high heat; stir until the meat is crumbly and has lost its pinkness and the onion is tender, about 7 minutes. Stir in the salt, chili powder and tomato sauce; keep hot. Shred the lettuce and arrange on individual salad plates. Top each with the meat mixture and sprinkle with cheese. Arrange on each salad tomato wedges and avocado slices, if used. Place corn chips around edges of salads and serve immediately. Makes 4 servings.

A Few Food Firsts for You

Frozen Coca-Cola is introduced.

We see the first all-plastic container for carbonated soft drinks hit the shelf this year.

Ever hear of Jonagold apples? This new variety is a cross of Golden Delicious and Jonathan, bred in New York. It is tangy, sweet, and great for cooking, baking, freezing, or just plain eating.

Proctor & Gamble researchers synthesize a fat substitute called sucrose polyester. The company ultimately coins the name "olestra" for its new product, which can be used to fry foods.

General Mills creates miniature boxes of Betty Crocker products for its "Easy-Bake" Oven.

The "Fun Size" Snickers candy bar hits the stores, becoming a favorite Halloween treat.

Kids love "Goober," Smucker's new striped peanut butter and jelly – all in one jar!

Hunt's Snack Pack comes out with pudding in single-serve aluminum cans.

Round Pringles Potato Crisps are housed in a unique cylinder-shaped can.

Hershey's Kisses come out in pastel blue, pink, and green foil for the Easter holiday. The Hershey Chocolate Company is renamed Hershey Foods Corporation this year.

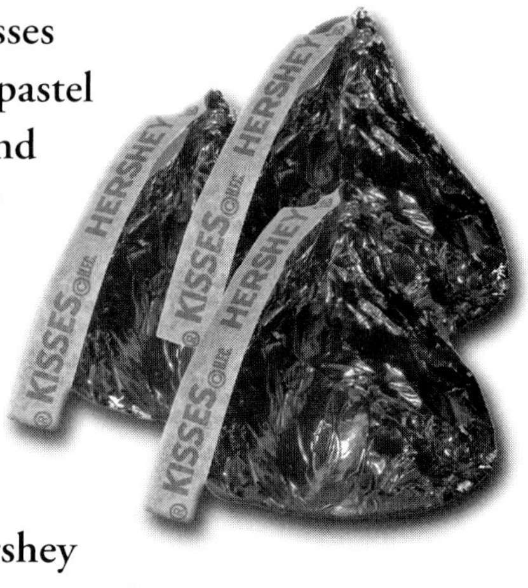

Fast Food Flair

The first **Roy Rogers Family Restaurant** opens in Falls Church, Virginia. The U.S. chain is named for cowboy actor **Roy Rogers**, and features roast beef sandwiches, fried chicken, as well as fast-food items like burgers and fries. The original restaurant serves "fast-food" fashion, but many franchises opt for the popular cafeteria style. All locations have the one most popular thing in common: the "fixin's bar," where patrons garnish their own sandwiches from a selection of ketchup, mayo, horseradish sauce, lettuce, tomatoes, pickles, onions, and the like.

The first **Red Lobster Restaurant** opens in Lakeland, Florida. The concept is simple: Great food at reasonable prices!

André Soltner becomes the first French chef outside of France to win the *Meilleur Ouvrier de France*, the highest French recognition for chefs.

Burger Chef, second only to McDonald's in number of locations across the East and West Coasts, is bought by General Foods Corporation.

International restaurateur Michael Chow opens his Chinese restaurant, Mr. Chow. In an effort to add sophistication to the genre, Chow serves in a European setting – including white tablecloths, Italian waiters, and high prices. "I wanted Chinese culture to have respectability and acceptance," Chow says.

Famous chef **Julia Child** publishes her second book, *The French Chef Cookbook* a collection of the recipes she has demonstrated on her television program, *The French Chef*. *TV Guide* states that although Child is not the first TV cook, she attracts the broadest audience – "from professors to policemen."

The term "Green Revolution" is first used by USAID Director William Gaud, who states, "The rapid spread of modern wheat and rice varieties throughout Asia and other developments in the field of agriculture contain the makings of a new revolution... I call it a Green Revolution based on the application of science and technology." "Green Revolution" is used to describe the agricultural transformation in developing nations, leading to increased production. Many claim that its major achievement is helping to avoid widespread famine, and that it is responsible for feeding billions of people.

• • •

For the first time, India produces enough grain to feed its 500 million people.

• • •

Sanitation requirements for food preparation are upgraded for meat, eggs, fish, and poultry. The Meat Inspection Act of 1906 is replaced by new, more stringent regulations in meat processing plants. Upton Sinclair, author of *The Jungle*, an exposé of the meat industry before 1906, is appropriately invited to the ceremonial signing.

• • •

Imitation foods are stealing some of the market away from their natural counterparts, particularly dairy products. Borden's milk substitute boasts more protein and less fat than milk, and imitation whipped cream, cheese, and margarine sales are rising. Artificial flavorings make bread taste better, meat flavors are added to sauces, and tomato and peanut imitation flavors hit the market.

Food prices increase about 5 percent since 1967, and some unhappy homemakers protest and picket supermarkets. Meanwhile, supermarkets begin decorating paper grocery bags with recipes and football schedules to draw consumers back to the same store every week.

• • •

Between 1968 and 1998, world food production increases by 84 percent, and food trade increases by 184 percent.

• • •

Plastic accounts for 95 percent of the packaging used for meat and produce. New York even passes a law requiring that all packaged meat be wrapped in clear plastic so buyers can really see what they're getting.

• • •

Meat and fish consumption in the U.S. is on the rise. The average American eats 105 pounds of beef, 63 pounds of pork, 46 pounds of poultry, 3.5 pounds of veal, and about 4 pounds of lamb this year.

• • •

As the aerosol can becomes popular, this year sees the birth of Pillsbury's cake decorator cans, canned cheese spreads, and even a gourmet spray for flavoring meats.

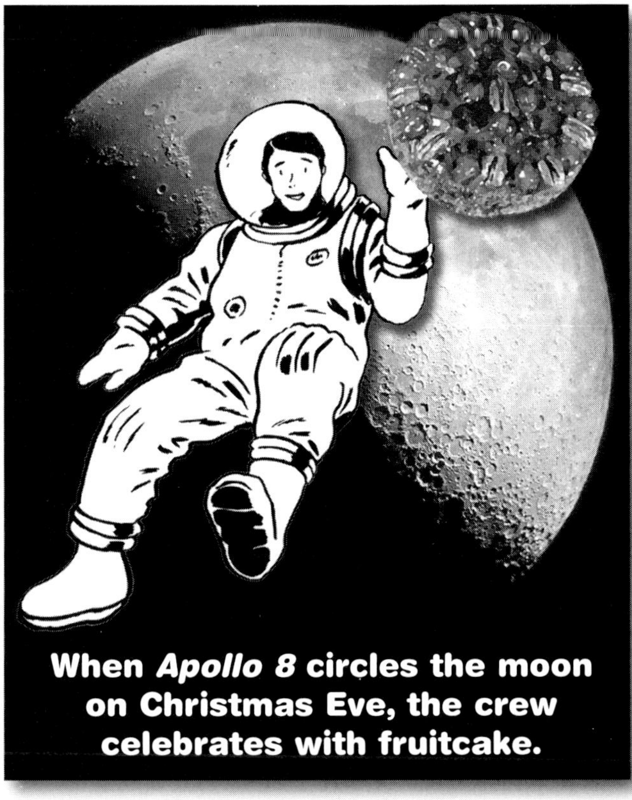

When *Apollo 8* circles the moon on Christmas Eve, the crew celebrates with fruitcake.

A six-pack of 10-ounce bottles of Pepsi goes for 59 cents.

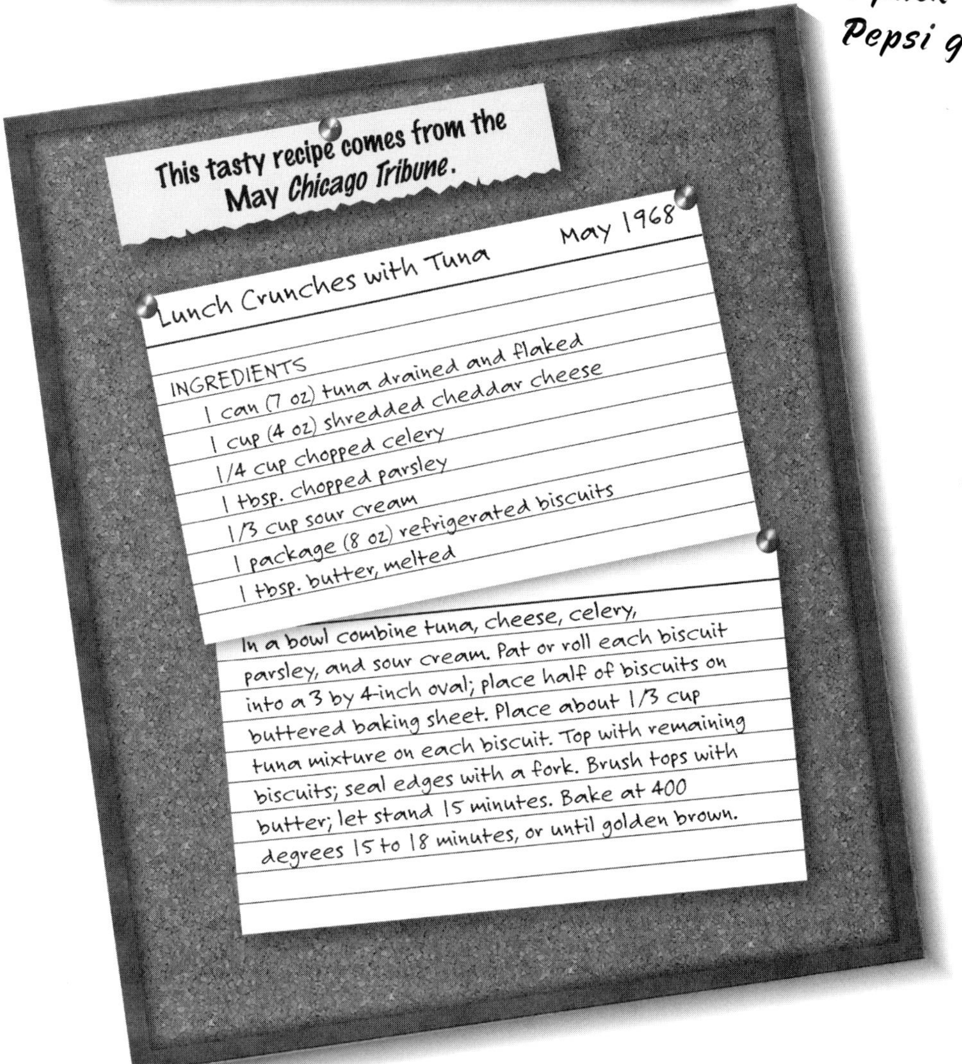

This tasty recipe comes from the May *Chicago Tribune*.

May 1968

Lunch Crunches with Tuna

INGREDIENTS
- 1 can (7 oz) tuna drained and flaked
- 1 cup (4 oz) shredded cheddar cheese
- 1/4 cup chopped celery
- 1 tbsp. chopped parsley
- 1/3 cup sour cream
- 1 package (8 oz) refrigerated biscuits
- 1 tbsp. butter, melted

In a bowl combine tuna, cheese, celery, parsley, and sour cream. Pat or roll each biscuit into a 3 by 4-inch oval; place half of biscuits on buttered baking sheet. Place about 1/3 cup tuna mixture on each biscuit. Top with remaining biscuits; seal edges with a fork. Brush tops with butter; let stand 15 minutes. Bake at 400 degrees 15 to 18 minutes, or until golden brown.

Soft drinks remain incredibly popular. The top sellers are the colas, and 15 percent of the market is claimed by low-cal versions. Interestingly, coffee consumption declines as soft drink sales climb.

1968 ADVERTISEMENT

Science

Apollo 7

On October 11, NASA launches *Apollo 7*, with the crew of Wally Schirra, Donn Fulton Eisele, and R. Walter Cunningham. This is the first manned Apollo mission, the first three-man American space mission, and also the first manned launch of the Saturn IB launch vehicle. Schirra is the only astronaut to have flown Mercury, Gemini, and Apollo missions. After the fire on the launchpad of *Apollo 1* the command module has been extensively redesigned. *Apollo 7* encounters no major problems and the mission is deemed a success.

Apollo 8

A Christmas Wish – From Space!

The successful flight of *Apollo 8* on December 24 makes Commander **Frank Borman**, Command Module Pilot **James Lovell**, and Lunar Module Pilot **William Anders** the first astronauts to orbit and see the far side of the moon, and planet Earth as a whole. Borman describes the moon as a "vast, lonely and forbidding sight," and Lovell calls the Earth "a grand oasis in the big vastness of space." As TV cameras transmit the first close-up images of the lunar surface, the astronauts read a Christmas message and all three take turns reading about creation from the book of Genesis.

William Anders: *"For all the people on Earth the crew of* Apollo 8 *has a message we would like to send you. In the beginning God created the heaven and the earth. And the earth was without form, and void; and darkness was upon the face of the deep. And the Spirit of God moved upon the face of the waters. And God said, Let there be light: and there was light. And God saw the light, that it was good: and God divided the light from the darkness."*

Jim Lovell: *"And God called the light Day, and the darkness he called Night. And the evening and the morning were the first day. And God said, Let there be a firmament in the midst of the waters, and let it divide the waters from the waters. And God made the firmament, and divided the waters which were under the firmament from the waters which were above the firmament: and it was so. And God called the firmament Heaven. And the evening and the morning were the second day."*

Frank Borman: *"And God said, Let the waters under the heavens be gathered together unto one place, and let the dry land appear: and it was so. And God called the dry land Earth; and the gathering together of the waters called the Seas: and God saw that it was good. And from the crew of* Apollo 8, *we close with good night, good luck, a Merry Christmas, and God bless all of you – all of you on the good Earth."*

The A.M. Turing Award

The A.M. Turing Award is given annually (by the Association for Computing Machinery) for lasting technical contributions made to the computing community. Most of the recipients have been computer scientists. This year, **Richard Hamming** wins the Turing Award for his work on numerical methods, automatic coding systems, and error-detecting and error-correcting codes.

1968 ADVERTISEMENT

Nobel Prize Winners

Luis Alvarez is the recipient of the Nobel Prize in Physics for "the discovery of a large number of resonance states, made possible through his development of the technique of using hydrogen bubble chamber and data analysis." His research makes it possible to record and study the short-lived particles created in particle accelerators.

Lars Onsager wins the Nobel Prize in Chemistry for his study of subatomic particles. Onsager was born in Oslo, Norway in 1903, moving to America in 1928. He holds honorary degrees of Doctor of Science from Harvard University, Rensselaer Polytechnic Institute, Brown University, Rheinisch-Westfahlische Technische Hochschule, and the University of Chicago.

Aha! People CAN Change!

A significant step in the world of cognitive science is made when **Anthony V. Manzo** demonstrates that reading comprehension can be dramatically improved through mental modeling, also known as cognitive apprenticeship training. Previously, reading comprehension was believed to be the best predictor of intelligence, and therefore unchangeable.

Earth-Saving Moves

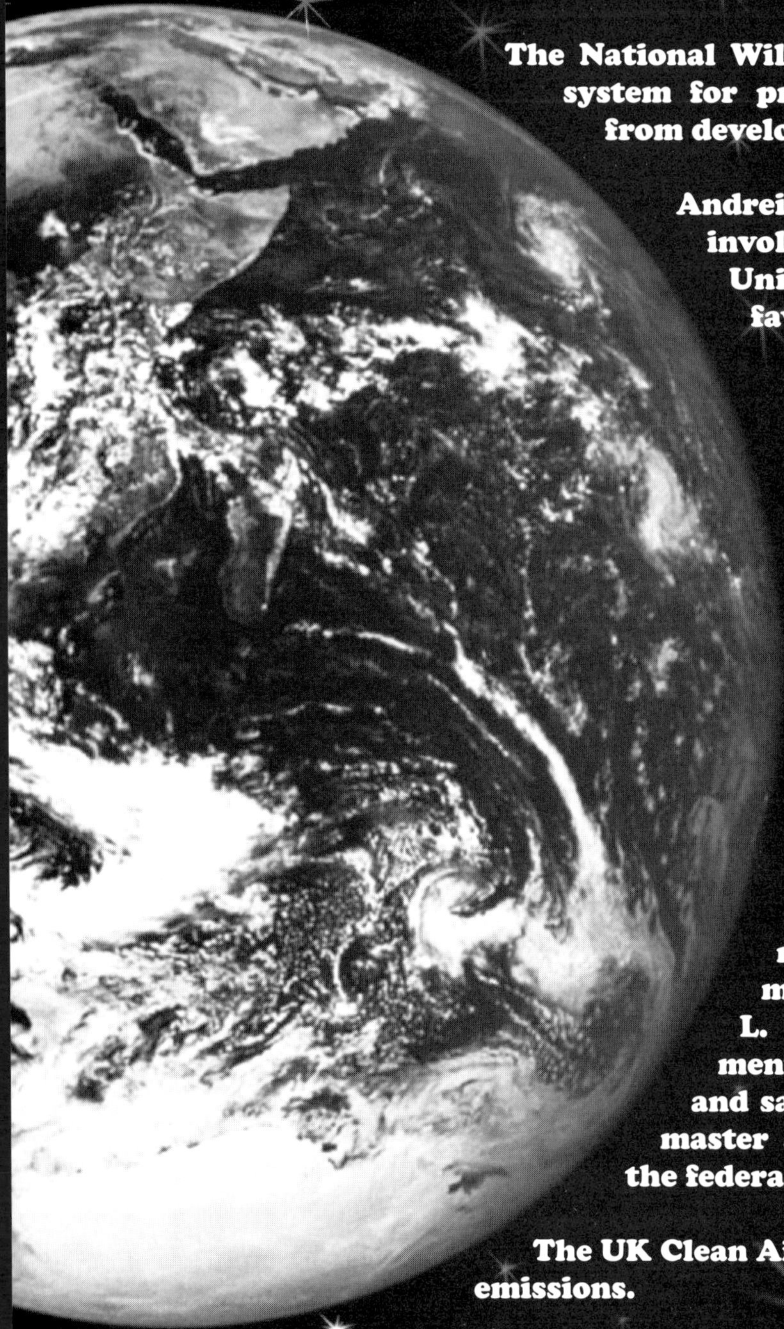

The National Wild and Scenic Rivers Act establishes a system for protecting pristine, free-flowing rivers from development.

Andrei Sakharov, a Soviet scientist who is involved with the development of the Soviet Union's hydrogen bomb, speaks out in favor of a reduction in nuclear weapons.

The Treaty on the Non-Proliferation of Nuclear Weapons (NPT) to limit the spread of nuclear weapons is signed on July 1.

The Ocean Drilling Program (ODP) is funded by the U.S. National Science Foundation and 22 international partners to research the history of the ocean basins and the overall nature of the crust beneath the ocean floor.

In July, the House and Senate spend a full day discussing the need for a national policy to protect the environment. Secretary of the Interior Stewart L. Udall tells Congress that his department has created the "Office of Ecology," and says it is time for Congress to "give this master science a new and central position in the federal scientific establishment."

The UK Clean Air Act increases restrictions on smoke emissions.

Got Gas?

The largest reservoir of American petroleum north of Mexico is discovered in Alaska.

A LITTLE SCIENTIFIC GENIUS GOES A LONG WAY...

Swiss biologist **Werner Arber** finds that bacteria defend themselves against viruses by cutting the virus DNA using special "restriction enzymes." These enzymes will later be widely used in developing DNA technologies.

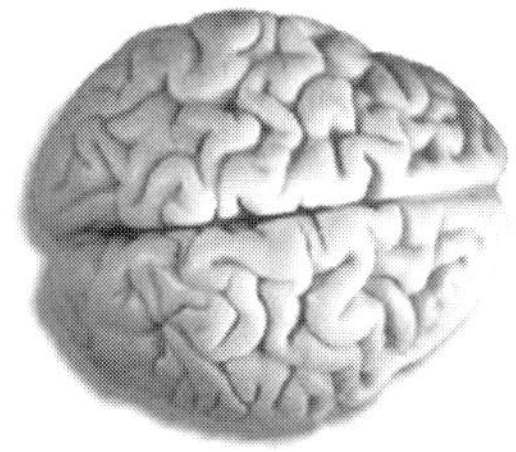

Norman Geschwind and **Walter Levitsky** show that there are differences in the sizes of the brain's hemispheres, and that the left hemisphere, associated with language, is larger 65 percent of the time.

Motoo Kimura formulates the neutral theory of evolution, stating that "almost all evolution at the molecular level is due to random drift, in contrast to neo-Darwinians who hold that natural selection plays the more prominent role."

Jürgen Habermas points out that "psychoanalysis consists of the hermeneutic interpretation of the complex text that is provided to the analyst by his subject," not the physics of the mind, as **Sigmund Freud** believes.

RCA devises a method for electronic control of light reflected from liquid crystals, demonstrating the first liquid crystal display (LCD). This discovery launches a global industry that will produce millions of LCDs for watches, calculators, flat-panel televisions, and computers.

UCLA physics and astronomy professor **Eric Becklin** identifies the center of the Milky Way.

Gabriele Veneziano introduces the String Theory, suggesting that "the big bang was not the origin of the universe but simply the outcome of a pre-existing state."

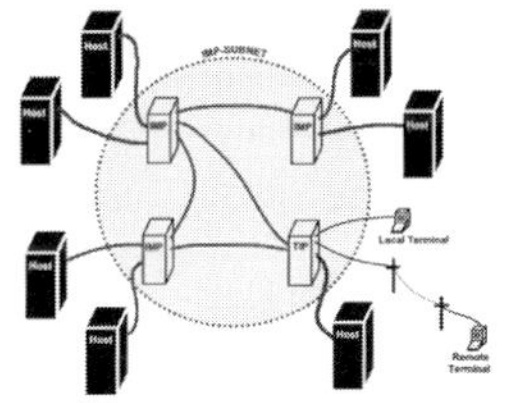

The ARPANET, predecessor to the Internet, is established by the United States Department of Defense Advanced Research Projects Agency (ARPA).

RESEARCH SHOWS...

DNA Dispute

James Watson publishes *The Double Helix*, relating how he and partner **Francis Crick**, both working from Cambridge University, beat their Oxford rivals to one of the most revolutionary discoveries in biochemistry – the structure of DNA (deoxyribonucleic acid). Watson's portrayal of the personal lives of those involved and the events leading to the discovery prove so controversial that Harvard University Press refuses to publish the book, considering its content to be "irreverent of the scientific research process."

Supersonic Speed in the Sixties

The Soviet-designed Tupolev Tu-144, the prototype of the world's first supersonic airliner, takes its maiden flight on December 31. It will first hit supersonic speed on June 5, 1969.

Population Prediction

Nobel Prize-winning immunologist **Paul R. Ehrlich** astounds us with his best-selling book, *The Population Bomb*. Ehrlich predicts disaster for humanity due to overpopulation and the "population explosion," stating that "in the 1970s and 1980s hundreds of millions of people will starve to death" and that "nothing can be done to avoid a mass famine greater than any in history."

Science Budget Cuts

When the government cuts $6 billion from the federal budget, **Donald F. Hornig**, President Johnson's science adviser, says "the new budget is going to cut not only into the fat, but also into the flesh of lots of areas, including science."

THERE'S A FIRST TIME FOR *Everything!*

Radio waves emitted by neutron stars, called pulsars, are discovered.

The term "tectonic plates" first appears in a journal article, rapidly replacing "continental drift."

An asteroid known as Icarus comes within 395,000 miles of Earth. Every 19 years this large asteroid swings by Earth, often coming within 4 million miles of the planet!

This year finds the earliest evidence of modern *Homo sapiens* in Africa when fossil remains dated more than 100,000 years old are recovered from a South African cave site by **J.J. Wymer.**

The recently discovered radio pulsars are explained by **Thomas Gold** as rapidly rotating neutron stars and subsequent observations confirm the suggestion.

DEATHS *in the* WORLD *of* SCIENCE

Russian physicist **LEV DAVIDOVICH LANDAU** dies at age 60.

German physicist and 1944 Nobel Prize winner **OTTO HAHN** dies at age 89.

American astronomer **HAROLD D. BABCOCK** dies at age 86. The Babcock crater on the moon is named for him, and asteroid 3167 Babcock is jointly named for him and his son, Horace.

Medicine

Marshall Nirenberg with molecular models in 1962.

The **Albert Lasker Award** for Basic Medical Research, also known as "America's Nobel," is one of the most coveted awards in medical science. Many Lasker winners do go on to win the Nobel, and this year is no exception. **Dr. Marshall W. Nirenberg** and **Dr. H. Gobind Khorana** proudly take the Lasker Award this year for their "outstanding achievements in deciphering the genetic code, thus revealing one of the most fundamental and intriguing secrets of life."

The **Nobel Prize** in Physiology or Medicine goes to three scientists "for their interpretation of the genetic code and its function in protein synthesis": **Robert W. Holley** of Cornell University, **Har Gobind Khorana** of the University of Wisconsin, and **Marshall W. Nirenberg** of the National Institutes of Health.

Nirenberg

Holley

Khorana

1968 Nobel Laureates at the awards ceremony.

THE WORD FROM THE WOMB

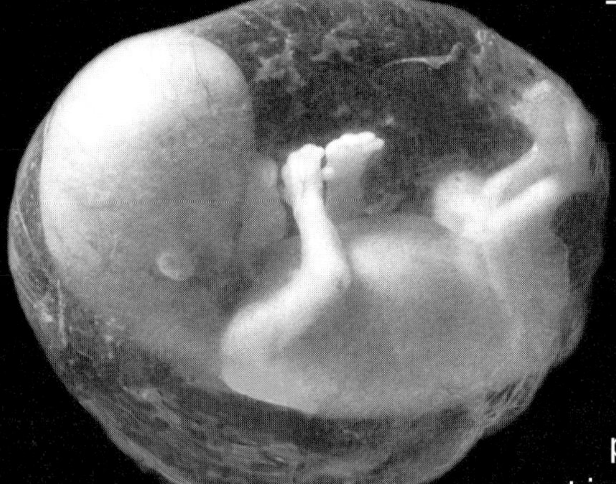

The third recipient of the 1968 **Lasker Award** is Professor **William F. Windle** for his research on the physiology of the embryo and the newborn, not only expanding knowledge of the major causes of cerebral palsy and mental retardation, but also pointing the way toward prevention and therapy.

Prenatal diagnosis begins to improve significantly, and cells from amniotic fluid can now be analyzed for chromosomal disorders like Down syndrome.

Chorionic villus sampling (CVS) is the taking of fetal tissue samples and analyzing them for chromosomal, biochemical, and DNA content. Jan Mohr's method of obtaining the sample via the cervix is abandoned because of its high rate of complications. By 1984, however, ultrasound-guided CVS sampling will be widely used.

Rh disease is one cause of hemolytic anemia in newborns, and can result in mild to severe anemia or even stillbirth. Problems can arise during pregnancy when mother and baby have different Rh factors (positive or negative) and the blood becomes mixed. In the early '60s two rival groups, American doctors John Gorman, Vince Freda, and William Pollack, and two Englishmen, Professor Cyril Clarke and Dr. Ronald Finn, almost simultaneously discover that by injecting the mother with an antibody against fetal red blood cells, the disease can be prevented. Approved in 1968 in England and the United States, the antibody is injected into more than 500,000 women, and *Time* magazine chooses it as one of the top 10 medical achievements of the 1960s. By 1973, it is estimated that over 50,000 babies' lives have been saved in the United States alone. In 1980 these five men each receive an Albert Lasker Award.

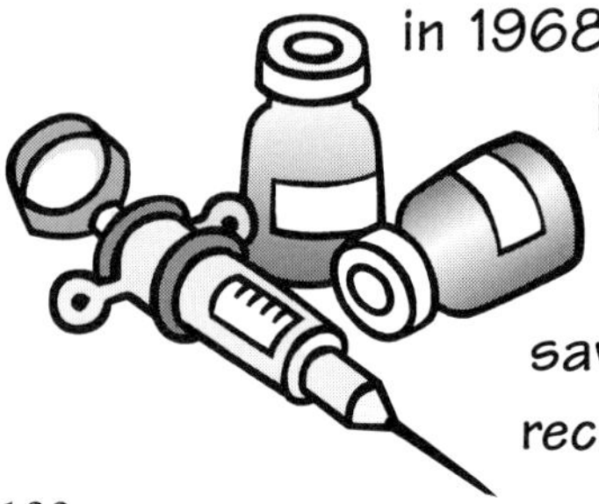

PROGNOSIS OF DISEASE

The National Advisory Cancer Council reports that "although research and educational activities on cancer have been greatly expanded, the number and rate of cancer deaths continues upward. However, the ratio of patients who survive 5 years or more following treatment, has improved from fewer than 1 in 5 thirty years ago to 1 in 3 today."

• • •

An experimental technique for diagnosing breast cancer, using an adaptation of the Xerox copying machine to photograph the breast, is reported by Dr. John N. Wolfe of Detroit.

Emphysema is the fastest growing killer in the U.S., quickly rivaling heart disease. Dr. E. Cuyler Hammond, Vice President of the American Cancer Society, tells the Senate Subcommittee on Air and Water Pollution that a combined atmosphere of cigarette smoke and pollution does, in fact, create a high risk for emphysema.

1968 ADVERTISEMENT

LEGALESE

The Social Security Administration tries to improve fiscal relations between hospitals and Medicare by establishing new payment procedures, and by proposing a 10 percent increase in the amount that must be paid before receiving Medicare aid. On December 31, Secretary of Health, Education and Welfare **Wilbur J. Cohen** blocks the increase.

• • •

Almost every American 65 years or older is covered by the basic hospital insurance plans under Medicare, and more than 90% sign up for the supplementary coverage. The premium for the supplementary insurance is increased from $3 to $4 per month.

• • •

Delaware becomes the fourth state to adopt a law requiring fluoridation of drinking water.

A Longer Life, A Better Life?

Cardiac surgeons work to become increasingly skilled at heart transplantation, despite claims that the operation does NOT promise long-term survival or a better quality of life. "There ensued what appeared to be an international race to be a member of the 'me-too' brigade. There has not been anything like it in medical annals," writes cardiologist **Irvine Page.**

Meanwhile, heart transplant surgery is performed on over 100 patients throughout the world this year. **Dr. Christiaan N. Barnard**, responsible for the first successful heart transplant in 1967, performs an even more successful transplant on January 2, and 58-year-old **Philip Blaiberg** is still doing well by year's end.

In January, heart surgery pioneer **Dr. Norman Shumway** of Stanford University Medical Center performs the first adult U.S. heart transplant. Shumway is also the only American surgeon to continue performing the operation after others stop due to poor results. Unfortunately, Shumway's transplant recipient, **Mike Kasperak,** dies after only 15 days.

Dr. Denton Cooley, the world-renowned surgeon who pioneered many techniques used in cardiovascular surgery, performs his first successful heart transplant in May. Cooley successfully transplants the heart of a 15-year-old suicide victim into a 47-year-old man, who survives for 204 days. Cooley will go on to perform 22 heart transplants over the course of the next year, at one point completing an incredible three transplants in five days. "There is no question in my mind that heart transplants can be done with very low risk – say, five percent mortality," says Cooley. "It will become a routine operation during the next decade. It's only a question now of resolving such details as body rejection and getting people to accept the idea of walking around with someone else's heart."

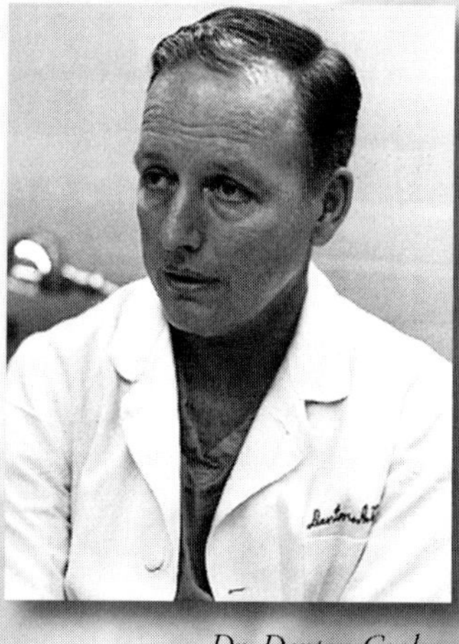

Dr. Denton Cooley

- In May, Britain's first heart transplant patient, **Frederick West,** dies 46 days after receiving his donor heart.

- Surgeons in Paris perform Europe's first heart transplant on **Clovis Roblain.**

- A doctor at the National Heart Hospital in London attempts the first transplant of a pig heart into a human, but the heart stops functioning minutes later.

DEATH REDEFINED

Transplant issues raise many ethical and legal considerations, and doctors and lawyers alike debate the issue of determining the exact moment of death. Doctors find that they can no longer pinpoint death as occurring within four to five minutes after heartbeat and breathing have stopped. Not all cells die simultaneously, and machines can keep the heart and lungs functioning even longer.

Liver transplants continue, but attempts at lung transplants fail.

World Medical Association (WMA) President says, "Doctors must never be in a position where it could be said that a donor was murdered to obtain an organ for a transplant." A Harvard study recommends that death be based upon a clearly irreversible coma, and that the patient be retested at least 24 hours later. Both Harvard and the WMA agree that the determination should be shared by at least two doctors, neither on the transplant team.

Dr. Lillehei of the University of Minnesota Medical School reports that four people suffering from severe diabetes have received the first pancreas transplants; three die, and the fourth is alive for a month at the time of the report.

The Ad Hoc Committee of the Harvard Medical School to Examine the Definition of Death redefines death to "include respirator-dependent patients who showed no signs of brain activity." John McCain, a North Carolina doctor, notes that human tissue supplies are like oil. "When first discovered, neither human tissue nor oil had been considered a natural resource, but thanks to technological advances, both became among our most precious resources." He then adds, "Before the capability of utilizing human tissue from one to help another was developed, human tissues were not considered a natural resource. In contrast to fossil fuel of which the supply is finite and the utilization rate is high, available human tissues for recycle use are bountiful but the utilization rate is low."

In May, the first transplant of a thymus gland is performed on a 7-month-old boy.

Nearly 200 heart transplants are attempted over the next few years, but most patients die within weeks. Although many surgeons back away from the procedure, state legislatures quickly adopt statutes establishing the legality of the commission's brain-death criteria. Under the resulting Death Act of the 1980s, a doctor can legally declare a patient dead using either the traditional criteria (irreversible cessation of circulatory and respiratory functions) or the new criteria of brain death.

A HEALTHIER AMERICA

Americans' health is better than ever, according to **Dr. Milford O. Rouse**, President of the AMA (American Medical Association). "Dramatic advances include progress in organ transplants, not only of the heart but also of the pancreas and liver." He also notes that mass inoculation has been so effective that "we may eliminate measles from the United States." Rouse also reports that the average hospital stay is the lowest in history, and the number of mental patients in hospitals is on a downward trend. Eating habits, however, are another story. The U.S. Department of Agriculture (USDA) reports that one household in every five eats a nutritionally "poor" combination of foods.

LONG-TERM VISION

Congress establishes the National Eye Institute, thus sealing a long-term commitment to protect the vision of the American people.

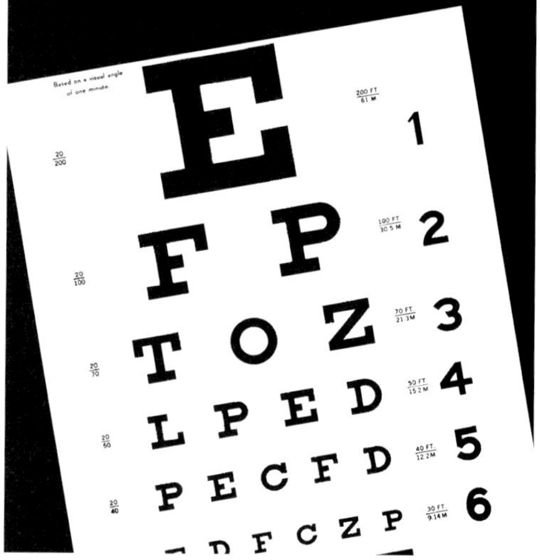

HERE'S TO YOUR EARS!

Studies at the University of Tennessee show that if you play rock music for a guinea pig at the normal sound level played in a discotheque, it will destroy cells in the critical cochlea of its ear. The study goes on to say that "the level of sound used by go-go bands is far in excess of the level that industry has been concerned about for years. We have apparently reached a point where the young people are losing sufficient hearing to jeopardize their occupational potential. We must enter into a program of safety or the consequences are going to be dire."

Dr. Sadek Hilal develops "embolization" to treat malformations of blood vessels in the brain by injecting substances to block them. This is the first step in developing "interventional radiology," and Dr. Hilal is considered one of the most influential researchers in imaging science and radiology over the past 50 years.

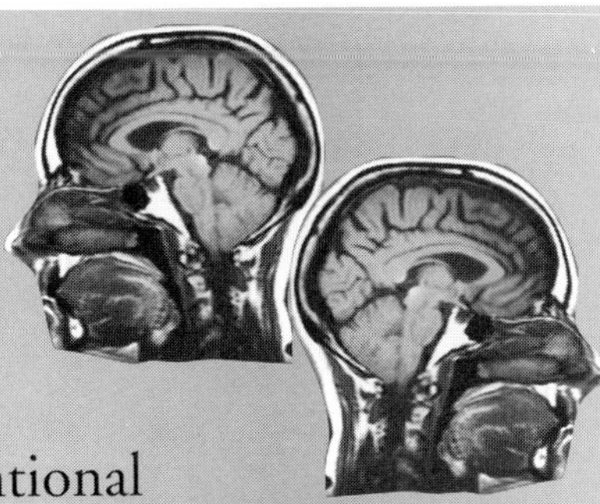

Psychosis Diagnosis

A chemical test to determine the severity of serious mental illness is reported to be up to 90 percent accurate in calculating the degree of psychosis in almost 400 patients!

GREAT NEWS FOR 'DENTAL PHOBES'

Dr. Seymour J. Kreshover, director of the National Institute of Dental Research in Maryland, predicts that tooth decay may be preventable in 10 years.

Despair Can Be Deadly

At the joint meeting for the American and Royal College of Physicians in London, Professor of Psychiatry Dr. **George Engel** reports a link between emotions and physical health. Engel says periods of "gloom, despair, grief and loneliness might predispose people to disease and aggravate their illnesses even to the point of death."

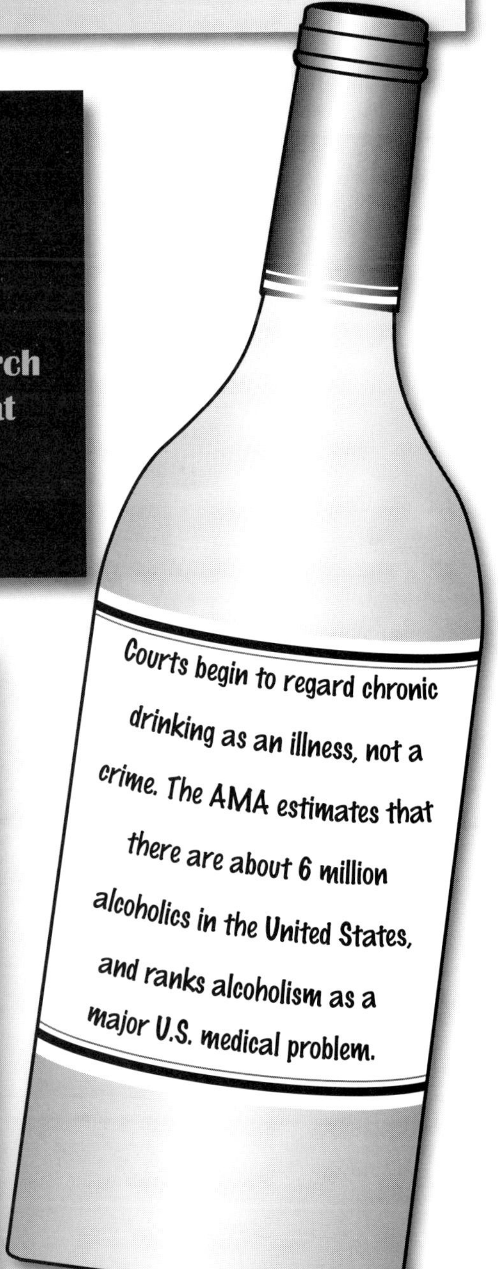

Courts begin to regard chronic drinking as an illness, not a crime. The AMA estimates that there are about 6 million alcoholics in the United States, and ranks alcoholism as a major U.S. medical problem.

1968 ADVERTISEMENT

You may never take a cold capsule again.

Vicks introduces NyQuil. A brand-new concept in colds medicines.

NyQuil is a nighttime colds medicine that relieves your major cold symptoms so well, it even helps you get the rest your body needs. So you'll feel better in the morning.

NyQuil doesn't relieve just a few cold symptoms as leading capsules do. NyQuil relieves sniffles, sneezes, a stuffy nose, scratchy throat, coughs, even minor aches and pains for hours. And because NyQuil is a liquid, you can feel it go to work faster, too.

That's why we figure you may never take a cold capsule again. Or a cold pill, either. Because, as you'll find out for yourself, new Vicks NyQuil is the one thing to take for your cold.

Vicks® and NyQuil® are registered trademarks of Vick Chemical Co., Div. of Richardson-Merrell Inc., N.Y., N.Y.

It's a Living

American consumers are borrowing more and saving less this year. Personal savings fall from 7.5% to 6.3% of after-tax income, and installment loans rise at a record annual rate of $9 billion! Credit is plentiful, mainly because the Federal Reserve Board is allowing the money supply to grow at an increasingly inflationary rate.

$ $ $

"Merger fever" seizes industry in the United States. Over 4,200 mergers take place this year, up 41% from 1967.

$ $ $

Trading on the New York Stock Exchange (NYSE) hits a record mark of 20.41 million shares on April 10.

$ $ $

The ACCRA (American Chamber of Commerce Researchers Association) cost of living index is created, touted as the most reliable source of city-to-city comparisons of key consumer costs anywhere.

$ $ $

The GNP (Gross National Product) grows by $70 billion to a total of $860 billion this year.

GOOD NEWS IN THE JOB MARKET

Along with a booming economy, employment grows by over a million, and unemployment rates drop to 3.8% – the lowest in 15 years! Of even more consequence, the number of people out of work for 15 weeks or more, the "hard-core unemployed," is down to 350,000 – 100,000 less than the previous year. Unemployment among adult white men is at 2%, and although the rate for blacks is higher, it is still down to a low of 6.5%. Wages rise, and the average hourly earnings of all workers in manufacturing hits a high of $3.05 in October.

$ $ $

KEEPIN' IT STEADY

With the buying power of the U.S. dollar a bit shaky, it may not be the wisest move when David M. Kennedy, Nixon's Secretary of the Treasury, refuses to pledge that the U.S. will maintain the official price of gold at $35 an ounce. "I want to keep every option open," he says. When the free market price of gold jumps to a six-month high the next day, Nixon Press Aide Ron Ziegler declares, "We do not anticipate any change in the price of gold." The international gold standard begins unraveling as interest rates start to rise and prices begin to take off. The two-tiered gold price system introduced this year ultimately leads to a complete abandonment of the gold standard a few years later.

$ $ $

HOW FAST CAN YOU SPEND IT?

Consumers are spending at record-breaking rates, with total personal consumption hitting $534 billion – over 8% more than in 1967. Prices for services are increasing the fastest, and 60% of all personal spending continues to go toward goods.

RISING COSTS:

Transportation 4.2%
Food 4.5%
Apparel 6.6%
Medical care 7.2%

According to Washington's economists, it now takes $122 to buy goods and services that cost only $100 a decade ago.

The federal minimum wage stands at 86% of the wage necessary to lift a worker and his or her family to the official poverty line for a family of four.

A HOSPITAL STAY COSTS $72 A DAY

The U.S. government's total purchase of goods and services is $197 billion, with $80 billion going for defense spending.

At the University of Michigan, the cost per credit is only $8.25.

Educational expenditures are up from $54.6 billion in 1967 to $58.5 billion this year.

The American Association of University Professors reports a 7.4% rise in salaries, but salary gains in the private sector rise much more slowly. Salaries of professors in public universities rise 8.1 percent, compared to 5.6 percent for their private counterparts. At Harvard University, the average full-time faculty salary is $19,300 – the highest in the country.

STATE OF THE STATS

Federal Spending:	$178.13 billion
Federal Debt:	$368.7 billion
Median Household Income:	$7,743
Consumer Price Index:	34.8
Unemployment:	3.8%
Dow-Jones High:	985
Dow-Jones Low:	825
Inflation:	4.2%
Unemployment:	3.8%

Corporate profits for the year are up to $91 billion. When a surcharge on income tax is proposed to offset the cost of the Vietnam War, it comes as no surprise that leaders of 13 corporations send wires to their congressmen encouraging its passage. It also comes as no surprise that the charge passes in June.

What Things Cost

Groceries, Etc.

Bacon (lb.)	$ .69
Bread, loaf	.25
Butter (lb.)	.80
Coca Cola (1 can)	.10
Eggs (doz.)	.53
Hot Dogs (lb.)	.59
Lettuce (head)	.19
Milk (gal.)	1.07
Salmon (lb.)	.88
Snickers Bar (large)	.15
Cigarettes	.50
First-class stamp	.06

The Working Man

Jeans	$ 4.00
Work Boots	20.00
Leather Belt	2.50
Fall Jacket	10.00
Suit	80.00
Dress Shirt	7.50
Ban-Lon Knit Sweater	13.00
Haircut	2.00
Old Spice Burley Aftershave	2.00
Refillable Butane Lighter	2.95
Timex Electric Wrist Watch	39.95

Around the House

Daily Newspaper	$ .15
Time Magazine	.50
Look Magazine	.50
Family Circle Magazine	.20
Encyclopedia Americana Set	375.00
Singer Vacuum Cleaner	88.00
Record Album	4.98
Go-Go Portable Phonograph	17.95
Polaroid Swinger Camera	24.95
Panasonic Stereo System	174.95
Admiral 14″ Portable Color TV	279.95
Singer Sewing Machine	149.95
Admiral Freezer/Refrigerator	399.95
Ecko Complete Set of Cookware	39.95
House	26,000.00

Out & About

McDonald's Burger	$ .25
McDonald's Big Mac	.49
Cup of Coffee	.20
Tap Beer	.25
Concert Ticket	5.00
First-Run Movies	3.00
Baseball Game Ticket	3.00
Bus Fare	.20
Gas (gal.)	.34
Toyota Corona	2,055.00
Volkswagen Squareback	2,349.00
Sears Radial Tire	45.08
Samsonite 26″ Suitcase	28.95
Hotel (Las Vegas Stardust)	8.00 - 10.00
Studio Condo in Aspen, CO	20,000.00

Diamonds Really Are This Girl's Best Friend!

*Jackie Onassis's wedding gift from husband **Aristotle** is valued at $1.2 million...a large ruby ring surrounded by large diamonds and matching earrings.*

Some salaries this year:

Senators, Members of the House of Representatives, and District Judges command about $30,000 a year.

Circuit Judges make $33,000.

Associate Justices, $39,500.

Chief Justice tops the list at $40,000.

This year 1/4 of New York's budget goes to welfare.

In contrast, the top-paid baseball player **Mickey Mantle** of the New York Yankees earned a whopping $100,000 this year!

LUCKY DOG!
A Florida heiress leaves $450,000 to 150 stray dogs.

When **Marvin Miller** was elected head of the Major League Baseball Players Association (MLBPA) in 1966, he transformed the organization into one of the strongest unions in America. By 1968, Miller succeeds in raising baseball's minimum salary from $6,000 to $10,000, clearing the way for enviably high baseball salaries.

On the international front, the Free World's Central Bankers have an emergency meeting in November with hopes of finding a solution to the threatened devaluation of the French franc.

The New York Hilton rents rooms on a "one-day by-the-hour plan" to make life easier for tourists: $12 for the first 3 hours and $3 for every hour after that.

IF IT WERE ONLY TRUE!

Based on current inflation trends, the Economic Unit of the *U.S. News & World Report* projects some costs for the year 2000.

	1968	2000
Day in Hospital (semi-private room)	$75	$630
New Car	$4,000	$9,900
Man's Haircut	$2	$10
Visit to the Beauty Salon	$12	$40
A Year in College (private)	$2,570	$6,000
A Year in College (public)	$1,600	$4,000
Having a Baby	$200	$640
A House	$40,000	$86,000
Family of Four Food (one week)	$40	$112
Man's Suit	$80	$270

There is good news on the horizon as well: the typical family income of $7,800 a year should increase to $36,000 by the year 2000.

The United Auto Workers' 1967 seven-week strike against tool shops in Detroit ends with an agreement of fringe benefits: a workweek of paid holidays from Christmas Eve through New Year's Day. It also provides a 95 cent per hour raise and increases of 25 cents over 37.5 months.

Social Security checks received in March this year will be at least 13% more. Even higher benefits await those not yet receiving Social Security, since the maximum earnings subject to Social Security tax is now $7,800, an increase of $1,200 from 1966.

PAY IS GOING UP... BUT TAXES ARE GOING WAY UP.

Average weekly earnings are increasing:

Factory Workers	$114.36
Retail & Wholesale Workers	$82.10
Insurance & Banking	$96.62
Miners	$135.93
Construction Workers	$153.36
Junior Executive	$288.46

A 6 percent raise this year won't go a long way due to higher federal taxes, higher Social Security and a higher cost of living. On average, a $300 raise for a factory worker making $5,000 per year will only net him $55; a $480 raise for a construction worker who earns $8,000 per year nets just $30; and a $900 raise for the junior executive earning $15,000 per year means just $27 extra at year's end.

FUTURE ENERGY PREDICTIONS

The Royal Dutch/Shell Group of oil companies in London reports that in the year 2000 the world will consume more than four times as much energy that is currently consumed. Oil and natural gas will produce 5% more energy than the 50% it is now producing, and coal will provide less energy in a larger market. Nuclear energy is set to soar to 18% of the energy produced, and half of the world's electrical-generating capacity will be nuclear. Much more oil and gas will be used for light fuels and chemical raw materials. Plenty of oil and gas remain in the ground, but the world will have to find it soon because by the year 2000 we will use half again as much oil and gas as has been found in the past 100 years.

Nervous Tension Takes Its Toll on American Workers

Dr. Joseph F. Montague

According to **Dr. Joseph F. Montague**, many American workers are suffering from a buildup of nervous tension. Most likely to be affected by the malady are those individuals who are "...the very sensitive, the very intelligent, the really worthwhile people in the world who do the things that make our civilization better and better as time goes on." Truck drivers are much less likely than executives to suffer nervous tension. Nervous tension can lead to stomach ulcers, colitis or heart attack, and the effects "...can be on any part of the body, but most particularly on the vital ones, the circulatory system, the digestive system and the mind."

In the workplace nervous tension can lead to poor judgment, poor concentration and unclear thinking. Those workers who are "capable of measuring up" to their jobs do not suffer from nervous tension, but those who are "inadequate" in their position suffer greatly. Overwork isn't a factor, but over-trying is, and one's ambition should match one's capabilities. A man should leave his domestic problems at home so as not to spread nervous tension throughout the office place.

Montague recommends that a person who suffers from nervous tension should drink an ounce of whiskey or rum with water before dinner, and create a regular schedule for themselves, by doing the same thing at the same time every day.

To avoid nervous tension Montague advises that a person should take frequent vacations, exercise, refrain from coffee, sleeping aids and overeating, smoke and consume alcohol only in moderation, and socialize on weekends and vacations, not during the workweek. Most importantly one should put one's problems in perspective and not exaggerate them. Montague states that the key is: "Don't let nothing bother you."

Teachers on Strike

This year, two leading United States teacher organizations expect 300 to 400 school strikes across the nation. Low salaries top the list of teachers' complaints. The annual salary for an elementary school teacher is \$6,700 - \$6,800. The average male teacher earns \$7,500, yet the Bureau of Labor Statistics "moderate standard of living basket" calls for \$9,200 for a family of four. Teachers are upset that they cannot live like a middle-class person even though on average they have been teaching for 12 years, are 39 years of age, are college graduates, and a quarter of all teachers have master's degrees. The BLS also states that from 1939 through 1967 the average public school teacher's salary has only increased 39.4%, yet a federal classified employee's salary has been upped by 56.8%, manufacturing employees are up by 101.1% and the per capita increase is 114.2%. Teachers are tired of moonlighting to make ends meet since most hold down at least one second job.

After World War II there was a large increase in the number of men who entered into the teaching profession. These men prove to be less tolerant of school deficiencies and more apt to complain to the school board about things like broken classroom windows, beat-up furniture, collecting milk money, supervising hallways or lunchrooms and keeping track of textbooks. School boards are trying to cut corners and save money, and not much is done to alleviate their concerns. Some teachers go to their state legislatures only to find more organized labor parties have been there before them, and there is little interest in their plight. Forced to fight for their jobs and schools in a way they know will get a response, they strike. For days and weeks across the country, schools are shut down. Mrs. Ruth Trigg, former head of the Classroom Teachers Association, sums it up best: "Perhaps the child's education will be interrupted for a week or a month, but what is one week or one month when measured against all the years of education, all less than adequate? If the teacher's militancy leads to improved conditions of learning, the child's opportunities are enhanced for a lifetime."

1968 ADVERTISEMENT

A NEW KIND OF CHAIR!

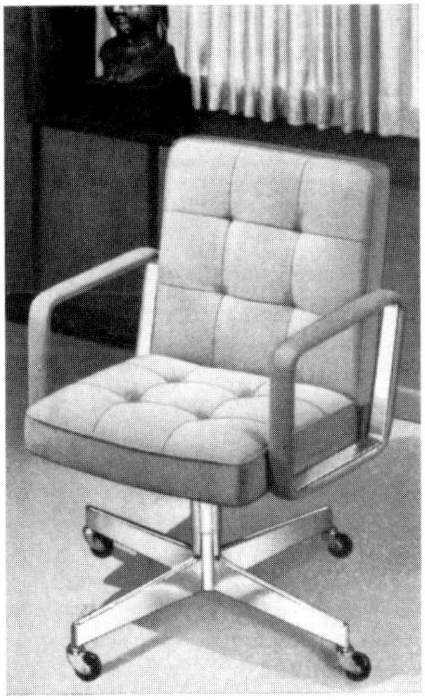

New looking. New sitting. An all-around *better* chair. In fact, a whole family of *thirty-two better chairs.*

All are handsomely styled and richly tufted. But *comfort*—there's the big difference. The all-new, heavily cushioned form-fitting Seats and Backs combine the softness you like with the day-long support you need.

That's why Shaw-Walker's new Duo-Synchro Chairs will help you feel better and work better.

See how easily you can have this beauty and comfort for every office worker. Phone your Shaw-Walkerman for the colorful chair brochure—*A Great New Concept.* It pictures all thirty-two design-coordinated models.

SHAW-WALKER

Largest Exclusive Makers of Office Equipment
48 Division St. Muskegon, Michigan 49443

IT'S O.K. TO CRY!?!?

TRW, a large California aerospace contractor, leads the way with innovative "Sensitivity Training" sessions for its executives. Called T-groups or encounter groups, this training is beginning to be offered by hundreds of companies nationwide. Small groups of executives spend up to three days together in sessions with a psychologist in an effort to discover how to create "helping relationships" between themselves. The focus of the group is on opening oneself to trust, expressiveness, caring, separateness, and empathy.

NEGATIVE INCOME TAX?

The Guaranteed Income (GI) movement is underway with 1,300 families in New Jersey and Pennsylvania. The concept is simple: pass tax money through the government and distribute it to low-income families. **Milton Friedman**, Senator **Barry Goldwater's** presidential campaign policy advisor, comes up with the most efficient way to pass the cash: Negative Income Tax. Low-income families would file income tax returns with the IRS, but instead of paying taxes based on the amount their income exceeds the tax liability threshold, they would receive payments from the IRS based on how far below the threshold they fall. The Negative Income Tax Experiment becomes a massive U.S. social experiment from 1968 to 1979, encompassing families from rural Iowa; rural North Carolina; Gary, Indiana, Seattle, Washington; and Denver, Colorado. Even today the idea still remains popular in some circles, but the Negative Income Tax system has never been implemented outside of the experiment.

1968 ADVERTISEMENT

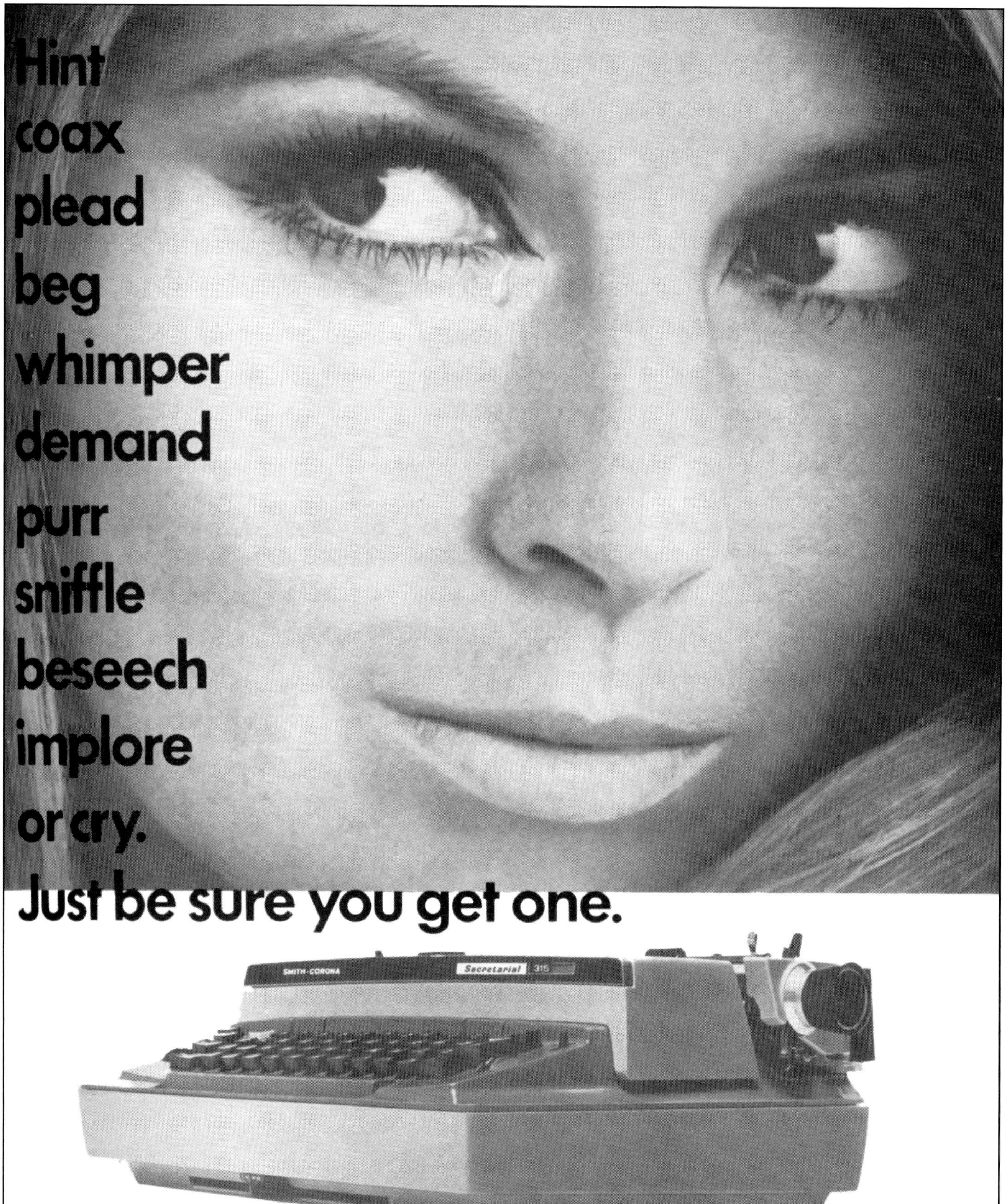

Fashion

HE ULTIMATE PARTY DRESS!

Norman Rockwell's portraits of the 1968 political contenders grace the fronts of these paper dresses made by James Sterling Paper Fashions, Ltd. Also available: a Rockerfeller shift and blazers for men.

Fashion

"Anything Goes" is fashion's statement this year. Skirts (and hair) get longer, leaving no doubt that the "hippie look" is in full swing. Women wear long, floor-length "maxi" dresses and skirts, as well as the ever-popular mini and even micro-mini. Minis have trouble with U.S. retail buyers, and designers quickly drop the hems for commerce. Minis are truly short-lived and all but vanish by the fall season shows. Although young Londoners still wear their skirts to mid-thigh, the trend is to just short of the knee. Mini designer Mary Quant is quoted as saying of the mini: "It is now a classic and therefore boring." Clothing is more fitted, and suit jackets are long, skinny, belted, and worn over slightly flared skirts. Tightly belted "happi" jackets are worn over shorts or slacks.

Hippy

***Hair*, the American "tribal love-rock musical" opens, celebrating long hair and permissiveness. Appliqued, crocheted, and knitted garments appear in ready-to-wear, and couture lines. Body art livens up any fashion, and makes it easy to change your wardrobe every day. Some stores offer the hand-painting of dresses or jewelry onto their clients.**

Cast from the musical *Hair*

Psychedelic jeans are created by outlining a design with a felt tip pen, filling it in with dye, and setting it with a cold water rinse.

Hippies are decorating everything, including painting their bodies.

Chic

The latest craze is decorating Levi's with unique crewelwork. The elementary stitches are so easy that anyone can do it.

Hit the discotheque in studded jeans, an American take on the English Cockney "pearly kings and queens."

Romance In The Air

Victorian is in, epitomized in ruffles, lace, and organdy of the bygone era. Pinafores are popular with top fashion designers **Geoffrey Beene, Oscar de la Renta,** *and* **Chester Weinberg***. The essence of romance is reflected in soft velvet pantsuits, frilly shirts, gold chains and baroque costume jewelry.*

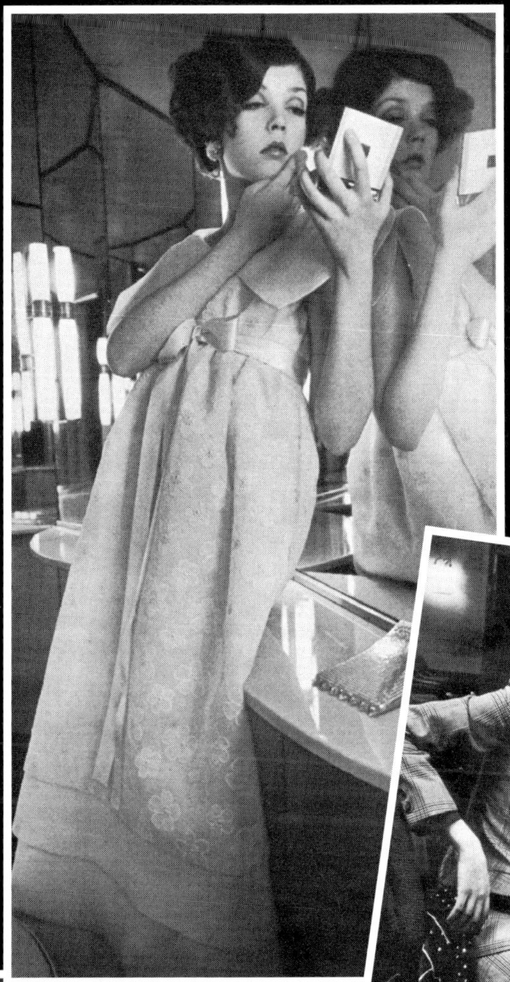

Actress Faye Dunaway is a fan of the latest Bonnie and Clyde look.

The film Bonnie and Clyde *brings a nostalgic fashion return to the late 1920s and early 1930s with cardigan jackets, berets, knotted silk scarves and jumpers. Also featured are midi-length (mid-calf) skirts, form-fitting ruffled shirts, bias-cut gowns and zoot-suit pantsuits. Make-up reflects the romantic styles of the '30s with red bow lips and dark lined eyes.*

Take a Peek!

The "body shirt" takes romantic fashion to a new level with sexy body-revealing shirts, see-through and worn over nothing, or unbuttoned and tucked! Designers go for the outlandish this year. Some of ***Yves St. Laurent's*** *designs are intentionally ostentatious, such as his see-through blouse under a maxi-length coat. St. Laurent, crowned "the little prince of couture" by the press, also brings Parisian chic to the safari suit.*

Betsey Johnson *attracts attention with gangster-stripe pantsuits and clear vinyl dresses with paste-on stars.* ***Rudi Gernreich*** *produces the world's first topless bathing suit, teams a strappy suit with high boots and a space visor, and also produces collections of see-through blouses and dresses. Plastic dresses with punched holes are shown by* ***André Courrèges. Geoffrey Beene*** *pairs short shirts with long jackets, and* ***Anne Fogarty*** *introduces her mini-culottes.*

Designer Kiki Byrne wears her own design out on the town, a see-through shirt in dotted swiss.

Feminists burn their bras at the 1968 Miss America pageant, and millions elect to go braless

Who needs buttons anyway?

Actress Barbara Feldon wears an opaque black chiffon shirt, white piqué bloomers, and ostrich earrings.

Surf's Up, Styles Are Hot!

From top left clockwise: The new Trikini, a two-piece top held by Velcro strips, for that "barely interupted" tan; three teeny-weeny triangles, the top two on a drawstring, the bottom one with knots on the sides; the *All Purpose T-Suit* goes under short skirts, or alone as a jumpsuit, cover-up, or sleepwear; and the Flower Power Bikini.

Ready for Women's Couture Pants?

Yves St. Laurent's wide-legged pantsuit, featuring a loosely belted tunic top and long, clinging jacket, combines comfort and femininity. "I am convinced that trouser fashions are truly the incoming way to dress," says St. Laurent. Although there is initial hostility among the press and buyers, the final orders for trouser suits and culotte suits represent a majority of the total buying at St. Laurent's fall-winter collection. Interestingly, many elegant restaurants continue to refuse service to trouser-clad females.

"Well, if you're asking me, I think it makes you look kind of effeminate."

A Look Magazine Cartoon from 9/3/68

Design by Yves St. Laurent

In her review of *The Why of Fashion* by **Karlyne Anspach**, *Guardian* writer **Alison Adburgham** says, "No one at this confusing point in fashion history would make predictions with any confidence. But I will hazard that when all the minis and maxis, the neo-1930s and the Victorian revivals have had their day, it may well be the casual yet well-groomed American way of dressing so fitted to modern life that will bridge the great divide now existing between young clothes and the rest."

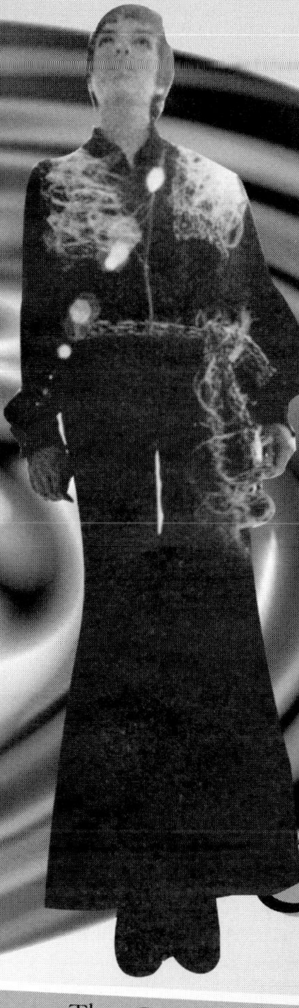

Bell-bottoms, long chains, belts, exotic feathers, laces and shiny, sexy fabrics complete the "Fashion Hippie" look many pop fashionists want. Liza Minnelli (right) wears her ostrich feather vest over black satin bell-bottoms and shirt. On left, the wife of Ahmet Ertegun (founder of Atlantic Records) wears a 6-foot chain made of Spanish coins to complement her look.

Patricia Shelton, fashion reporter for the *Christian Science Monitor*, writes, "Any genius can put a wardrobe together – all it takes is an artist's eye for color, line, and rhythm; confidence; a little common sense and a good credit rating. Prices are going up." A writer for *English Vogue* adds, "Fashion is self-consciously sociological and frankly feather-brained. It's classic and immediate. Nostalgic and now. Worldly and other-worldly. Whatever's happening you are part of it and at last you can be yourself and look as you choose."

Panne velvet is also big this year. "The kids have been wearing [panne velvet] in tenth-hand dresses to Chelsea parties and now it's abundant in both couture shows and in our manufactured clothing," writes London's **Serena Sinclair.**

The **Coty American Fashion Critics' Awards** are often referred to as the Oscars® of the clothing world. This year, **Giorgio Sant'Angelo** wins the award for his avante-garde accessories; **Bill Blass** for his menswear; **Oscar de la Renta** and **Bonnie Cashin** take the *Return Award*; and **George Halley** and **Luba of Elite** are awarded the *Winnie*, which is the award given to the leading designer of American women's fashions.

1968 ADVERTISEMENT

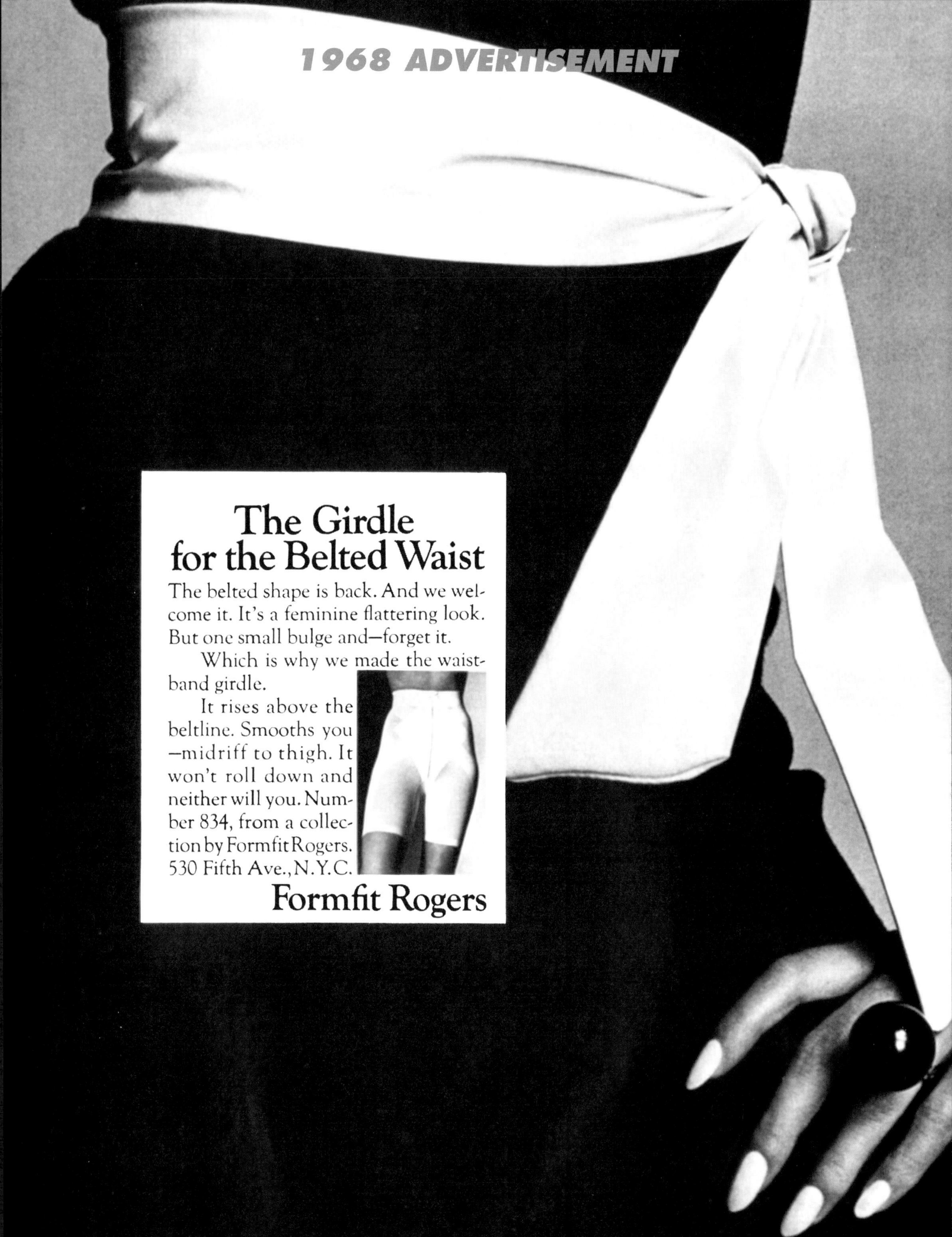

SPACE-AGE SILVER

This is the year the "space-age" look really takes off following the success of *Barbarella*. **André Courrèges'** designs feature silver and white PVC, "moongirl" pants in silver, white catsuits, and striped monochrome mini-skirts. His zip-fronted bolero jacket with hipster trousers is also a favorite.

Andre Courreges shows a client his $395 plastique raincoat at one of his chain of stylish 'Couture Future' boutiques.

WIDE BELTS

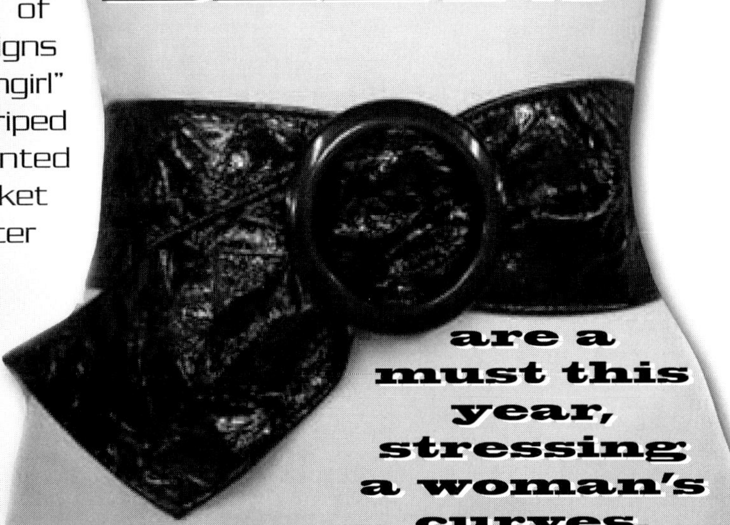

are a must this year, stressing a woman's curves.

DOES ONE SIZE FIT ALL?

British firm **Pretty Polly** announces "the stretchiest stockings and panti-hose yet, resulting from a new concept of hosiery manufacture, which are marketed in one standard size and guaranteed to fit all normal dimensions." The conversion of women to panty hose continues with constant technological improvements to the garments. **Wolford,** an Austrian company, introduces their first suspenderless stockings. The adjustable support tops are designed so the hose will fit most sizes of legs.

SHINY, SPARKLY, SEQUINS!

Sequin trimmings grace the Paris collections, and whether they are large or small, sequins make the scene at classy parties and discotheques alike.

"The tennis sweater gathers sequins and goes to the Opera. The riding habit takes a skirt and goes to lunch at Le Pavillion," writes yet another New York reporter.

MR. BLACKWELL'S WORST DRESSED LIST OF 1968

Jane Fonda

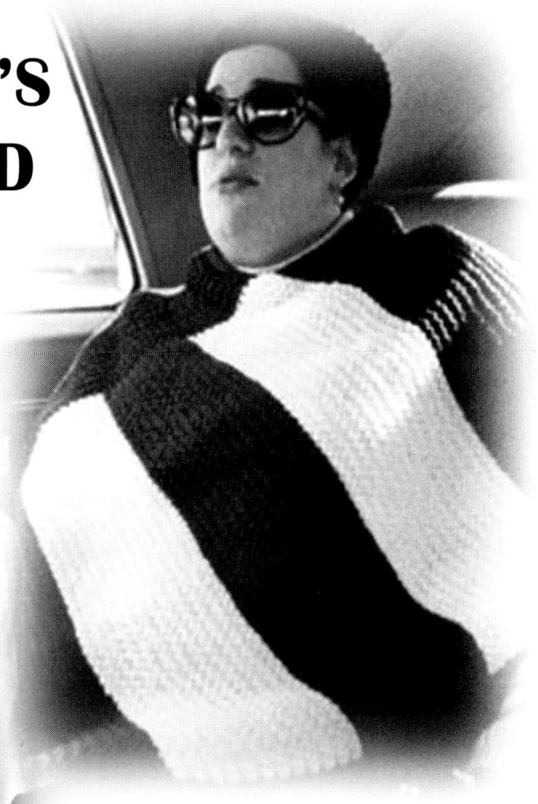

Mama Cass Elliot

Raquel Welch

Doris Day

Julie Andrews

Carol Burnett

Lennon Sisters

Kaye Ballard

Brigitte Bardot

Vanessa Redgrave

Designer Buzz

Geoffrey Beene creates suit jackets with padded hips, the first since figures went out of fashion in favor of the "Twiggy" look. He pairs short shirts with long jackets.

Laura Ashley opens her first shop in Kensington this year. She's known for her country-style clothing that she introduced in 1961.

Paco Rabanne, the son of **Cristobal Balenciaga's** head seamstress, designs jewelry and accessories for Paris couturiers such as **Balenciaga** and **Dior**. Rabanne designs **Jane Fonda's** wardrobe for the film *Barbarella*, and becomes known for his "chain-mail style," made from plastic and metal tiles or discs held together with wire. By 1968, his designs include ostrich feather dresses with aluminum bodices, paper, and silver leather.

Women adore the 36-year-old Italian **Valentino Garavani's** designs, and now men can too when he opens his *Valentino for Men* boutique this fall. Italy's "golden boy" of couture is a favorite of the jet-set crowd, and fashion-conscious women like **Jacqueline Kennedy** will fly to Rome just to pick up their Valentinos.

Anne Klein launches *Anne Klein & Company*. Her goal is to design and market sophisticated sportswear as coordinated separates. She comes to define how American sportswear is worn and sold. Anne Klein will be presented with two Coty Awards and named to the Coty Hall of Fame. Klein dies unexpectedly in 1974 at the age of 50.

With his wide tie designs and a $50,000 loan, **Ralph Lauren** founds *Polo Fashions*. In addition to clothing, his line will ultimately feature furniture, bedding, drapes, towels, rugs, china, silverware, and even potpourri.

Before forming her own fashion house this year, **Zandra Rhodes** had already designed a paper wedding dress that sold for less than two shillings! Rhodes and **Sylvia Ayton** open the *Fulham Road Clothes Shop*, becoming known for "fantasy evening fashions" in outrageous patterns and bright colors, as well as printed and painted silk and chiffon garments with art deco motifs. Rhodes' line clearly personifies the psychedelic "flower power" culture of the '60s.

Inspired by the unpretentious style of New York's youth, American fashion designer **Calvin Richard Klein** sets out to launch his own clothing company. Childhood friend **Barry Schwartz** provides the financial backing, and Klein hires a local seamstress to make some coat and dress samples. Within weeks of a Bonwit Teller merchandise manager's visit to Klein's showroom, the store buys $50,000 worth of merchandise. *Calvin Klein Ltd.* is born, and the line highlights clothing and accessories with simple, elegant lines and luxurious materials. His elegant designs, paired with linen, silk, and cashmere in neutral earth tones, create a look of careless good taste.

Sonia Rykiel first attracts the attention of the fashion gurus with her unusual sweaters. Her style becomes very popular with the American stores, and women appreciate her relaxed style.

Designer **Norman Norell** markets the *Norell* perfume, the first *Revlon* fragrance named after a designer.

Fashionable

Body Sculpture

Accessories

Beads

Wood Beads

Button Beads

Pumps

Gold Lurex

Christian Dior

Exotic Textures

Ostrich Feathers

Snake Skin

Funky Boots

Ankle Go-Go

Mid-calf Go-Go

Lace-up Woven Leather

Open Toe Lace-up Go-Go

Last season's boots are back and are all the rage. The hottest style from New York is a two-tone, two-material design, hitting either the knee or the hip. The most fashionable shoes are cut high on the foot, have a chunky high heel and are highly decorated. Toes are broad and rounded. Italian styles continue to control the market, bringing more and more minor style adjustments and rendering last year's fashions with side stitching obsolete. Evening footwear is dominated by stiletto heels, the later the evening — the higher the heel.

HAIR trends

Paul Mitchell as he styles model Jane Hitchcock's wig.

Mia Farrow in "Rosemary's Baby."

Vidal Sassoon is the top name in hairdressing. In fact, when **Mia Farrow** wants her hair styled for *Rosemary's Baby,* she pays $5,000 to fly him to the set!

Paul Mitchell comes from the ultra-hip Sassoon school of hair-styling and runs the shop at **Henri Bendel**, a top New York hair salon. Mitchell partners with **John Paul DeJoria** in 1980 forming **John Paul Mitchell Systems.**

Curls, which appear early in the year, falter and all but disappear by fall shows. Paris stylists propose the "apple head" style—round, smooth and shiny. New York, London, and Rome happily follow Paris' lead, with a trend toward helmets, hoods and snoods.

Most African Americans stop using chemicals to straighten their hair, resulting in the "Afro" hairstyle. The look catches on with both white and Japanese contemporaries. Black soul stars like **Sly of Sly and the Family Stone** sport the most spectacular Afro styles, supporting the new "Black is Beautiful" fashion statement.

MEN'S FASHION

Men continue to grow their hair longer and longer, and even the most conservative seem to be wearing colors and clashing patterns they would have shied away from earlier. While the turtleneck and pendant is common for casual wear, the Nehru jacket quietly fades into oblivion. One U.S. formal wear company offers to exchange the Nehru suits for more traditional counterparts. Surprisingly, the Edwardian look takes off in high fashion and business suits. Fashion photographers like Britain's **Patrick Lichfield** are combining "flower power" with a "dandy" image. **Bill Blass, Oleg Cassini, John Weitz** and **Valentino** usher in coachman's lapels, trapezoid pocket flaps, capes, capecoats and black velvet suits.

Versatile Italian artist Beni Montresor goes with the Edwardian look.

Turtlenecks are are a popular choice for casual wear styles.

American artist Andy Warhol favors the pop fashions with his velvet pants, ruffled and lace-trimmed dinner shirt, with belts and chains to accessorize.

OFF THE RACK

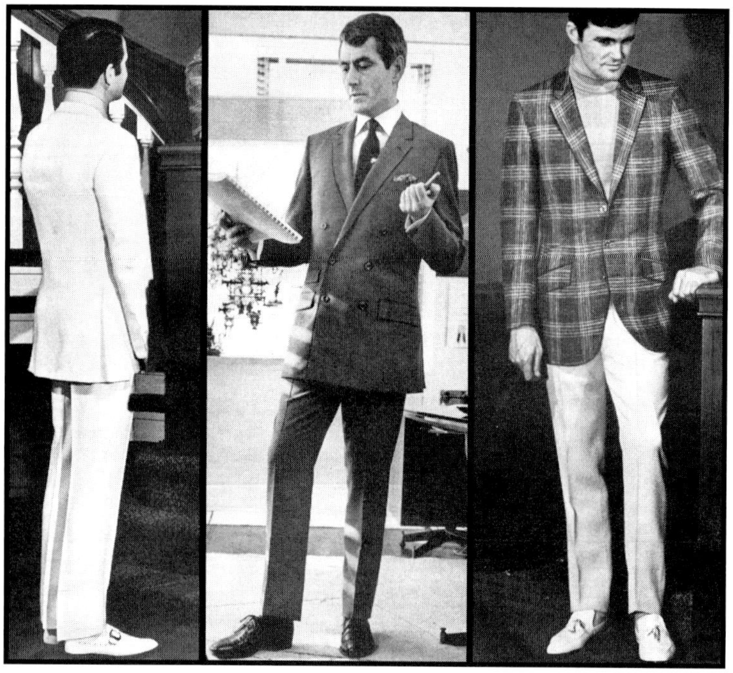

A new line from English designer **Hardy Amies** creates a tailor-made look at ready-made prices for American consumers. He states that "there are so many bright young executives on their way up. They need clothes that can help them – at a price that won't hurt." His trademark fashion is the deeply vented, slightly flared jacket. His casual styles include jackets made of brown and orange glen plaid, paired with a turtleneck, white wool pants and white shoes.

1968 ADVERTISEMENT

Sports

1968 OLYMPICS

Sports

Summer Olympics

The 1968 Summer Olympics, officially known as the Games of the XIX Olympiad, are held in Mexico City October 12–27.

The choice to hold the games in Mexico City is controversial for several reasons. Only 10 days before the games open, the Mexican army surrounds a group of students protesting against the government. When they open fire, 267 are killed and 1,000 are wounded. The tragic event comes to be known as "La matanza de Tlatelolco" or the Tlatelolco Massacre.

In addition, the country's high altitude sparks debate. While the thin air does hurt athletes in endurance events, it also leads to world records in all the shorter races, as well as the long jump and triple jump. **Avery Brundage**, IOC President, states, "The Olympic Games belong to all the world, not the part of it at sea level."

Al Oerter

Outstanding American performances include **Al Oerter's** record fourth consecutive discus title and **Debbie Meyer's** three gold medals for swimming.

Debbie Meyer

The unpredictable **Dick Fosbury** wins the high jump by jumping over the bar backwards and headfirst, forever known as the "Fosbury flop."

Dick Fosbury

Bob Beamon's spectacular long jump of 8.90 meters beats the old record by 63 centimeters, and will hold the world record for 22 years. **Wyomia Tyus** becomes the first woman to win back-to-back gold medals in the 100-meter dash.

Bob Beamon

Enriqueta Basilio

Mexican hurdler **Norma Enriqueta Basilio de Sotelo** becomes the first woman to light the cauldron at the Opening Ceremony.

Eulalia Rolinska of Poland, **Gladys de Seminario** of Peru and **Nuria Ortiz** of Mexico are the first women to compete in shooting.

The sports pages this year serve as quite a reflection of the racial antagonism in the United States. When a moderately successful black boycott of the New York Athletic Club's indoor meet at Madison Square Garden is held, other boycotts for the Olympic Games are threatened. The International Olympic Committee (IOC) votes to allow South Africa to compete in the 1968 Olympics in Mexico City. When 32 African nations announce their withdrawal from the games over the course of only three weeks, the IOC reverses its decision and again bans South Africa due to its apartheid policies.

On October 15th, ***Tommie Smith*** *of San Jose State College sets a world record in the 200-meter dash. Australian Salvation Army worker* ***Peter Norman*** *comes in second, and* ***John Carlos*** *of San Jose State takes third place. On the victory stand, Smith and Carlos wear black knee-length socks and one black glove. In recognition of Smith's victory, the two black Americans stand with heads bowed and gloved fists raised—in the world-recognized sign for "we shall overcome." Smith tells the media that he raised his right fist to represent black power in America, while Carlos' raised left fist represents unity in black America—together forming an arch of unity and power. Smith's black scarf stands for black pride, and the black socks represent black poverty in racist America. Declaring that they had "profaned Olympic principles by advertising their domestic political views," the Olympic Committee strips them of their credentials and gives them only 48 hours to leave Mexico. The committee states: "The basic principle of the Olympic Games is that politics plays no part whatsoever in them. U.S. athletes violated this universally accepted principle...to advertise domestic political views."*

Earlier in the year, San Jose State teacher ***Harry Edwards*** *campaigned for black athletes to boycott the Olympics. "What does it profit the black man to win a gold medal if when he comes home he is still a nigger?" In the end, Edwards failed to gain the support of the black athletes and the boycott never materialized.*

The most popular female athlete of the games is Czech gymnast **Vera Caslavska**, who takes four gold and two silver medals. Just two months before the Olympics, the Soviet's invade Czechoslovakia. Caslavska's resistance toward Soviet involvement in her homeland put her in danger of being arrested and she went into hiding. In the mountains of Czechoslovakia, she kept in shape by practicing her floor exercise in a meadow and swinging from tree limbs. After three weeks she was allowed to join the rest of her team in Mexico City.

Vera Caslavska

These Olympic Games see the first drug disqualification, when **Hans-Gunnar Liljenwall,** Swedish entrant in the modern pentathlon, tests positive for alcohol. Liljenwall claims to have had "two beers" to calm his nerves before the pistol shooting portion of the pentathlon. Nevertheless, the Swedish team eventually has to return their bronze medals.

TOP 3 NATIONS

	GOLD	SILVER	BRONZE	TOTAL
1 USA	45	28	34	**107**
2 USSR	29	32	30	**91**
3 JAPAN	11	7	7	**25**

The Mexico City Olympics are the first Summer Games to include sex testing for women.

Winter Olympics

Thirty-seven countries participate in the Winter Olympics in Grenoble, France February 6–18.

Jean-Claude Killy

France's **Jean-Claude Killy** sweeps the men's Alpine events, but the games are marred by rival **Karl Schranz's** claim that a mysterious man in black crossed his path during the slalom race, causing him to skid to a halt. Schranz beat Killy's time on retart, but a Jury of Appeals disqualified Schranz for missing two gates and gave the victory to Killy. Ultimately, the French team finishes fourth, and Killy becomes the first skier to win all three Alpine events since 1956.

Karl Schranz

Another controversy comes to a head in the women's luge when the three East German entrants, who had finished first, second and fourth, are disqualified for heating the runners of their sleds.

Peggy Fleming

Peggy Fleming wins the only United States gold medal in women's figure skating.

ABC's extensive coverage of Fleming and Killy makes the winter games more popular than ever in the U.S.–especially among teenage girls this year!

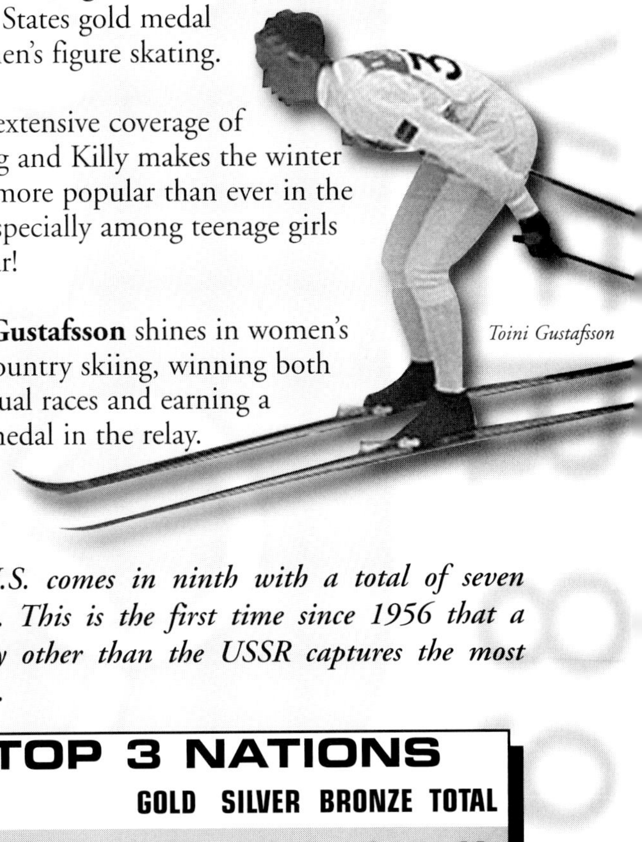

Toini Gustafsson

Toini Gustafsson shines in women's cross-country skiing, winning both individual races and earning a silver medal in the relay.

The U.S. comes in ninth with a total of seven medals. This is the first time since 1956 that a country other than the USSR captures the most medals.

TOP 3 NATIONS

	GOLD	SILVER	BRONZE	TOTAL
1 NORWAY	6	6	2	**14**
2 USSR	5	5	3	**13**
3 FRANCE	4	3	2	**9**

This year marks the first time the IOC allows East and West Germany to enter the games separately, and the first time the IOC orders drug and gender testing.

BATTER UP!

Mickey Lolich

Pitcher **Mickey Lolich** of Detroit allows just five runs in three complete games, winning all three including the final and decisive game—remaining the last pitcher to win three complete games in a single World Series. **Denny McLain** becomes the first pitcher in Major League Baseball to win 30 or more games since **Dizzy Dean** of the St. Louis Cardinals back in 1934. This year is remarkable for McLain as he is an All-Star, wins the Cy Young Award, and wins the American League's Most Valuable Player Award.

Tiger's catcher Bill Freehan makes the final out of the Series, then catches Mickey Lolich as he jumps into Freehan's arms.

The **Detroit Tigers** take the World Series 4 to 3 over the **St. Louis Cardinals**.

PLAY BALL!

PITCHERS DOMINATE THE GAME THIS YEAR with Detroit Tiger **Denny McLain** and St. Louis Cardinal **Bob Gibson** leading their teams to the World Series. L.A. Dodger **Don Drysdale** breaks **Doc White's** 64-year major league record when he pitches six consecutive shutouts. In May, **Jim "Catfish" Hunter** of the Oakland Athletics pitches the 10th perfect game in major league history in a game against the Minnesota Twins. **Tom Phoebus** of the Baltimore Orioles throws a 6–0 no-hitter against the Boston Red Sox at Baltimore's Memorial Stadium. St. Louis Cardinals pitcher **Joe Hoerner** ties a National League record for relievers with six consecutive strikeouts vs. the New York Mets. Chicago White Sox relief pitcher **Wilbur Wood** ends his season with a 7–6 win over the California Angels—a major league record 88 appearances!

The July 9th **All-Star Game** at the Houston Astrodome is the first ever to be played in an indoor arena and on artificial turf. The **National League** defeats the **American League** 1–0, and again, pitching dominates the game. **Willie Mays** (taking the place of an injured **Pete Rose**) scores the game's only run in the first inning and takes the Most Valuable Player award.

Willie Mays

The batting average of both leagues is at an all-time low. **Frank Howard** of the Washington Senators shines as one of hitting's few bright stars when he sets a new record, hitting 10 home runs in six consecutive games.

COLLEGE BALL

University of Southern California beats **University of Southern Illinois** 4–3 to win the National College Baseball Championship. USC's **Bill Seinsoth** is this year's College World Series MVP.

The first basic agreement between players and owners is ratified. The agreement runs from January 1, 1968 to December 31, 1969. The minimum major league player's salary is raised to $10,000. Meal money is up from $12 to $15 a day, and players will get $40 a week for training-camp expenses—up from $25.

Baseball's Opening Day on May 9 is postponed because of the funeral for the **Rev. Dr. Martin Luther King, Jr.** The next day, **Hubert Humphrey** throws out the first ball to start the Washington Senators vs. Minnesota Twins game, while soldiers patrol the streets around the D.C. stadium to prevent rioting.

William D. Eckert is dismissed as Baseball Commissioner by major league owners, serving three years of his seven-year contract.

Although attendance in the American League is up a bit, National League attendance drops by over a million.

Hank Aaron becomes the eighth player in major league history to hit 500 career home runs.

Jim Bunning's first win with the Pittsburgh Pirates at Dodger Stadium is also his 40th career shutout and includes his 1,000th National League strikeout. Bunning is the first pitcher since Cy Young with 1,000 in each league.

Roger Maris hits his 275th (and last) regular-season home run.

In September, **Gaylord Perry** of the San Francisco Giants pitches a no-hitter at San Francisco's Candlestick Park as the Giants beat the Cardinals 1–0. A mere 16 hours pass by before **Ray Washburn** of the St. Louis Cardinals evens the score making major league history with his second consecutive no-hitter in the same park.

Carl Yastrzemski goes 0 for 5, maintains his .301 batting average, and wins his second straight batting crown with the lowest winning average ever.

Hall of Fame

Goose Goslin, born Leon Allen Goslin, and **Hazen Shirley "Kiki" Cuyler** are admitted to the Hall of Fame by unanimous vote of the Special Veterans Committee.

Joseph Michael Medwick, nicknamed "Ducky," is voted into the Baseball Hall of Fame by the Baseball Writers Association of America. In his time, Medwick played for the St. Louis Cardinals, Brooklyn Dodgers, New York Giants and Boston Braves.

Awards

Most Valuable Player

Denny McLain
Detroit Tigers (AL)
Bob Gibson
St. Louis Cardinals (NL)

Cy Young Award

Denny McLain
Detroit Tigers (AL)
Bob Gibson
St. Louis Cardinals (NL)

Rookie of the Year

Stan Bahnsen
New York Yankees (AL)
Johnny Bench
Cincinnati Reds (NL)

DOWN AND DIRTY

Former major league player and manager Lena Blackburne dies. Blackburne, the source for mud used by umpires in both leagues to rub down new balls, leaves the mud business to childhood friend John Haas. "There's something about this mud," says retired major league umpire Bill Kinnamon. "I don't know how to explain it. It takes the shine off without getting the ball excessively dark."

Hank Aaron

PRO FOOTBALL

Vince Lombardi retires as head coach of the **Green Bay Packers. Phil Bengtson** takes his place and the Packers have a disappointing season with 6 wins, 7 losses and 1 tie.

The AFL sees the creation of a new expansion team, the **Cincinnati Bengals,** with **Paul Brown** as head coach. They finish their first year 3–11.

The AFL divisional playoff sees the **Oakland Raiders** win 41-6 over the **Kansas City Chiefs**. But the **New York Jets** with quarterback **Joe Namath** take the Championship game from them 27–23. In the NFL divisonal playoffs the **Baltimore Colts** take the **Minnesota Vikings** 24–14, and the **Cleveland Browns** conquer the **Dallas Cowboys** 31–20. In the NFL Championship game the Colts slaughter the Browns 34-0. The Colts and Jets head for Super Bowl III.

Chicago Bear Dick Butkus (#51).

Cleveland Brown Frank Ryan launches the ball.

Most Valuable Player
NFL **Earl Morrall** Baltimore Colts
AFL **Joe Namath** New York Jets

Rookie of the Year
NFL **Earl McCullough** Detroit Lions
AFL **Paul Robinson** Cincinnati Bengals

The Bert Bell Award
Leroy Kelly Cleveland Browns

NFL Coach of the Year Award
Don Shula Baltimore Colts

N.Y. Giant Fran Tarkenton (#10) and Cleveland Brown Bill Glass.

L.A. Ram Deacon Jones hits Dallas Cowboy Leon Donohue.

SUPER BOWL II

Super Bowl II is played on January 14th at the Orange Bowl in Miami, Florida. The NFL champion, the **Green Bay Packers,** defeats the AFL champion, the **Oakland Raiders,** 33–14. This only furthers the belief of most fans and sportswriters that the top NFL teams are superior to the top AFL teams.

Packers coach Vince Lombardi is carried off the field in one of Super Bowl history's most memorable images.

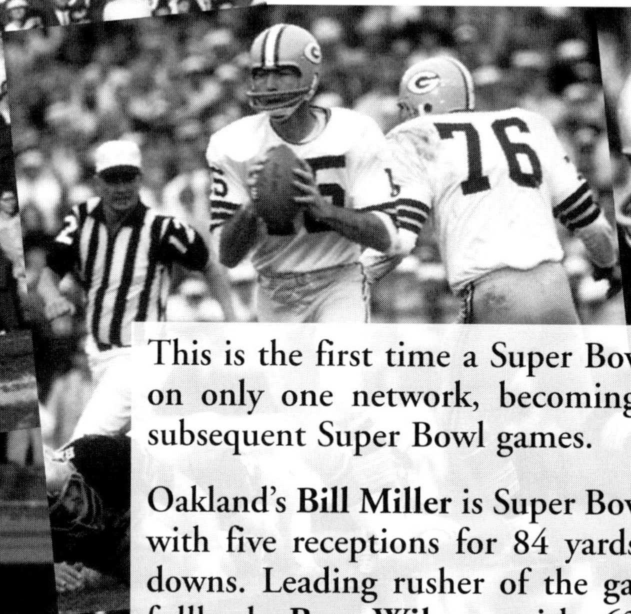

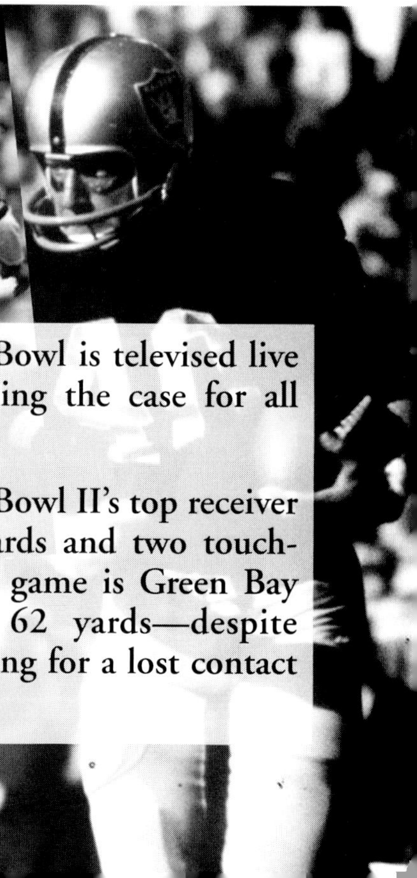

This is the first time a Super Bowl is televised live on only one network, becoming the case for all subsequent Super Bowl games.

Oakland's **Bill Miller** is Super Bowl II's top receiver with five receptions for 84 yards and two touchdowns. Leading rusher of the game is Green Bay fullback **Ben Wilson** with 62 yards—despite missing part of the game looking for a lost contact lens on the sidelines!

COLLEGE FOOTBALL

Rose Bowl
USC 14 - Indiana 3

Sugar Bowl
LSU 20 - Wyoming 13

Cotton Bowl
Texas A&M 20 - Alabama 16

Orange Bowl
Oklahoma 26 - Tennessee 24

USC halfback and Heisman Trophy winner **O.J. Simpson** dominates the college football season, finishing with a record of 1,709 yards.

Gator Bowl
Missouri 35 - Alabama 10

National College Football Champion
Ohio State

A YEAR OF NICKNAMES

West Texas State halfback
Eugene "Mercury" Morris

USC halfback
Orenthal James "The Juice" Simpson

Coach of the Year
Woody Hayes
Ohio State

Oregon State fullback
Bill "Earthquake" Enyart

U of Miami's defensive end
Ted Hendricks: "The Mad Stork"

Southern Methodist University's **Chuck Hixson** leads all passers, completing 265 of 468 passes for 3,103 yards and 21 touchdowns.

Ken Crots of Toledo sets a National Collegiate Athletic Association (NCAA) record by making 64 points in a row.

PRO BASKETBALL

MAKING HEADLINES

In the 1967–1968 Championship Series, the **Boston Celtics** beat the **Los Angeles Lakers** 4–2, claiming their ninth championship in 10 years.

Wilt Chamberlain (7 feet, 1 inch tall) of the 76ers is named NBA Most Valuable Player for the third straight year, setting an all-time career scoring record of 25,434 points.

The first season of the newly formed American Basketball Association (ABA) ends when the Eastern Division champion **Pittsburgh Pipers** defeat the western division champion **New Orleans Buccaneers** 4 games to 3 in the ABA Playoffs.

Rookie of the Year: **Earl Monroe** of the **Baltimore Bullets**

Dave Bing (#21)

Leading Scorer: **Dave Bing** of the **Detroit Pistons**

The 1968–69 season sees the **Los Angeles Lakers** make news by trading for **Wilt Chamberlain**. By adding Wilt to a lineup that includes future Hall-of-Famers **Elgin Baylor, Jerry West** and **Gail Goodrich**, the Lakers feel confident about capturing their first NBA title, after many years of being runner-up. The heavily favored Lakers cruise through the season and playoffs to set up a showdown with the **Boston Celtics** in what will be one of the most memorable NBA finals. The Celtics stun the basketball world by pulling out the upset victory by a mere two points in the decisive 7th game, which also marks the last game for **Bill Russell**.

Wilt Chamberlain

BASKETBALL

UCLA BRUINS

Legendary Coach **John Wooden** leads the UCLA Bruins in an incredible season. On January 20th they face the University of Houston at the Astrodome in the historical "Game of the Century," the first NCAA regular season game that is televised nationwide in prime time. Going in with a two-and-a-half season, 47-game winning streak, they suffer their only loss of the season in an upset 71–69. Despite the loss, the NCAA Championship is theirs for the taking. In the playoffs they rip through New Mexico State, Santa Clara University and the University of Houston, this time crushing them 101–69. The Bruins face the University of North Carolina for the NCAA Championship game. UCLA's lineup includes **Lew Alcindor** (now Kareem Abdul-Jabbar), **Lucius Allen, Mike Lynn, Mike Warren** and **Lynn Shackleford**. Alcindor scores an impressive 34 points during the game and receives the Most Outstanding Player award. UCLA easily wins the NCAA Championship with a score of 78–55. This is the Bruins' fourth national championship and they are the first team to twice win back-to-back NCAA titles.

HOCKEY

The National Hockey League doubles from six teams to 12 for the 1967–1968 season.

In the Eastern Division, the **Montreal Canadiens** take first place, edging out the **New York Rangers**. In the Western Division, the **Philadelphia Flyers** take first place by a single point, beating the **Los Angeles Kings** 73–72.

Montreal Canadiens

Stan Mikita, center for the **Chicago Black Hawks,** wins the **Art Ross Memorial Trophy,** his fourth leading scorer title in five years. **Phil Esposito** of the **Boston Bruins** comes in second; he is followed by **Gordie Howe** of the **Detroit Red Wings**.

Stan Mikita

STANLEY CUP
The **Montreal Canadiens** beat the **St. Louis Blues,** taking the Cup for a record 14 times!

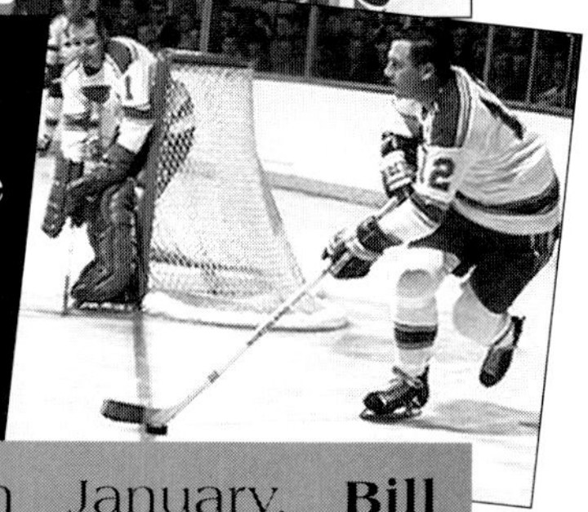

Hart Memorial Trophy
Stan Mikita *Chicago Black Hawks*

Lady Byng Memorial Trophy
Stan Mikita *Chicago Black Hawks*

Calder Memorial Trophy
Derek Sanderson *Boston Bruins*

James Norris Memorial Trophy
Bobby Orr *Boston Bruins*

Bill Masterson Memorial Trophy
Claude Provost *Montreal Canadiens*

World Hockey Championship
Soviet Union defeats **Czechoslovakia**

NCAA Championship:
University of Denver Pioneers
defeat
University of North Dakota Fighting Sioux
4–0

In January, **Bill Masterson** of the Minnesota North Stars suffers the first fatal injury in the NHL's history. Masterson is not wearing a helmet when he falls and hits his head on the ice. To honor his memory, a moment of silence is observed during the all-star game. The Professional Hockey Writers' Association sets up an annual award to memorialize Masterson and to honor his dedication to the sport. The Bill Masterson Memorial Trophy is given at the end of each season to the National Hockey League player who best exemplifies qualities of perseverance, sportsmanship and dedication to hockey.

BOXING NEWS

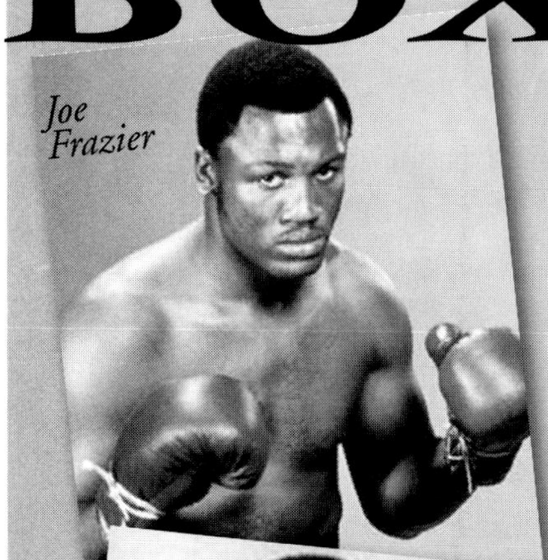
Joe Frazier

Nino Benvenuti

Bob Foster

Lionel Rose

Stripped of his World Boxing Association heavyweight title and his license to fight in 1967, **Muhammad Ali** is appealing his conviction for draft evasion and cannot fight in the U.S.

In March, **Joe Frazier** knocks out **Buster Mathis** to grab the heavyweight title in Illinois, Maine, Massachusetts, New York and Pennsylvania. The following month in Oakland, California, **Jimmy Ellis** wins the WBC heavyweight title.

Italy's **Nino Benvenuti** regains the middleweight title, and **Bob Foster** of Washington, D.C. wins the light heavyweight crown.

The lightweight title goes to **Carlos "Teo" Cruz**, the featherweight title to **Jose Legra**, and the bantamweight title to Australian **Lionel Rose**.

BORN IN 1968

MARY LOU RETTON
American gymnast

TONY HAWK
American skateboarder

JEFF BAGWELL
American Major League baseball player

FRANK THOMAS
American Major League baseball player

BARRY SANDERS
American pro football player

DARRIN VAN HORN
American boxer

SAMMY SOSA
American Major League baseball player

• • •

PASSINGS

JESS WILLARD
American heavyweight boxing champion

BILL MASTERTON
Canadian ice hockey player

DUKE KAHANAMOKU
American swimmer and surfer

JIMMY CLARK
Formula One racing driver

1968 ADVERTISEMENT

Men's Golf

Billy Casper

The year's best golfer is **Billy Casper** of San Diego, California, winning 6 tournaments and leading the money winners with over $205,000.

Arnold Palmer becomes the first golfer to reach $1 million in earnings over the course of his career.

Roberto de Vicenzo

Bob Goalby wins the Masters Tournament in Augusta, Georgia. **Roberto de Vicenzo** of Argentina ties Goalby, but improperly marks his card during the tournament, losing his chance for a playoff.

Lee Trevino wins the 68th U.S. Open in June in Rochester, New York.

Newcomer **Tony Jacklin** becomes the first English player in 48 years to win a PGA event, the Greater Jacksonville Open.

Tony Jacklin

Forty-eight-year-old **Julius Boros** of Ft. Lauderdale, Florida, wins the PGA Championship with a score of 281, one better than Arnold Palmer.

Gary Player of South Africa wins the British Open for the second time; his first was in 1959.

Gary Player

Bob Goalby

CYCLING

Tour de France
Jan Janssen
Netherlands

Giro D'Italia
Eddy Merckx
Belgium

World Cycling Championship
Vittorio Adorni
Italy

CYCLING

Women's Golf

Carol Mann

Kathy Whitworth of Texas and **Carol Mann** of Maryland dominate women's golf this year, each winning 10 of 32 tournaments. Whitworth sets a new one-year earnings record for women of $48,379...the 4th year in a row she leads the money winners!

Susie Maxwell Berning of Incline Village, Nevada takes the U.S. Open in July with 289.

Canadian rookie **Sandra Post** becomes the youngest female golfer to ever win a PGA major tournament by capturing the LPGA Championship.

TENNIS

Nancy Richey

Rod Laver

The "Open Era" in tennis begins, and for the first time amateurs and professionals compete against each other. By year's end, every prominent pro is beaten at least once by an amateur player.

The three leading players are Professional **Rod Laver**, amateur **Arthur Ashe** and Registered Player **Tom Okker**.

Laver wins his 3rd Wimbledon title, and earns more than $60,000 this year. He's also chosen as the world's top player by a panel of experts named by *World Tennis Magazine.*

Ashe wins the U.S. amateur title, becoming the first U.S. player to win the title since 1955, and the first black player ever to win. Two weeks later, he becomes the first amateur to win an open in the U.S. Open at Forest Hills.

Davis Cup of world tennis: United States defeats Australia 4-1.

Arthur Ashe

MEN'S TENNIS GRAND SLAM

Australian Open - **Bill Bowrey**
French Open - **Ken Rosewall**
Wimbledon Championship - **Rod Laver**
U.S. Open - **Arthur Ashe**

WOMEN'S TENNIS GRAND SLAM

Australian Open - **Billie Jean King**
French Open - **Nancy Richey**
Wimbledon Championship - **Billie Jean King**
U.S. Open - **Virginia Wade**

Virginia Wade

ICE SKATING

Olympic champion **Peggy Fleming** wins her 3rd straight women's world figure skating championship in Switzerland. **Emmerich Danzer** of Austria also wins his 3rd world title. The Pairs are won for the 4th time by **Ludmilla Belousova Protopopov** and husband **Oleg**.

Miwa Fukuhara of Tokyo takes the women's pro ice-skating title at the Wembley Empire Pool in London in April.

SPEED SKATING

Per Willy Guttormsen of Norway breaks the world 10,000-meter record—time is 15 minutes, 16.1 seconds.

Stien Kaiser of the Netherlands sets a new world record for women's 1,000-meter with a race time of 1 minute, 31 seconds.

Auto Racing

INDIANAPOLIS 500:
Bobby Unser (Robert William Unser) is one of seven drivers to win the Indianapolis 500 three times, and one of only two to win it in three different decades (1968, 1975 and 1981).

STOCK CAR RACING:
Cale Yarborough beats **LeeRoy Yarbrough** by one second to win the 10th Daytona 500.

NASCAR CHAMPIONSHIP:
David Pearson, known as the "Silver Fox," debuted on the Grand National racing circuit in 1960, earning Rookie of the Year. He wins the NASCAR Championship in 1966, 1968 and 1969, earning the reputation as one of the greatest of all NASCAR drivers.

MONTE CARLO RALLY:
Vic Elford and **David Stone** win the rally driving a Porsche 911T.

DRAG RACING:
Don "Big Daddy" Garlits wins the NHRA Top Fuel Championship.

FORMULA ONE CHAMPION:
Graham Hill of Great Britain

24 HOURS OF LE MANS:
The team of **Pedro Rodríguez** and **Lucien Bianchi** wins in a Ford GT-40.

HORSE RACING

The *Morning Telegraph* and *Daily Racing Form* vote four-year-old Tartan Stable's **Dr. Fager** Horse of the Year: Dr. Fager wins seven of the year's eight races.

Dancer's Image overtakes **Forward Pass** to win the 94th Kentucky Derby. However, several days later the horse is disqualified after traces of phenylbutazone, a painkiller much like aspirin, are found in the horse's urine.

Forward Pass wins the Preakness, and **Stage Door Johnny** takes the Belmont Stakes.

In the world of harness racing, **Nevele Pride** is voted Horse of the Year.

In September, **Cardigan Bay** becomes the first harness horse to hit $1 million in earnings.